EDITIONS

ARMENIAN
BULGARIAN
BURMESE (Myanmar)
CHINESE
DUTCH
ENGLISH
  Africa
  Australia
  Chinese/English
  India
  Indonesia
  Japan
  Korean/English
  Korean/English/
    Japanese
  Myanmar
  Philippines
  Singapore
  Sri Lanka
  United Kingdom
  United States
ESTONIAN
FRENCH
GREEK
GUJARATI
HINDI
HUNGARIAN
IBAN/ENGLISH
ILOKANO
INDONESIAN
ITALIAN
JAPANESE
KANNADA
KOREAN
MALAYALAM
NEPALI
NORWEGIAN
ODIA
POLISH
PORTUGUESE
  Africa
  Brazil
  Portugal
RUSSIAN
SINHALA
SPANISH
  Caribbean
  Mexico
  South America
  United States
SWEDISH
TAMIL
TELUGU
THAI
URDU

D0794810

THE UPPER ROOM

WHERE THE WORLD MEETS TO PRAY

Sarah Wilke
Publisher

INTERDENOMINATIONAL
INTERNATIONAL
INTERRACIAL

33 LANGUAGES
Multiple formats are available in some languages

The Upper Room
January–April 2016
Edited by Susan Hibbins

The Upper Room © BRF 2016
The Bible Reading Fellowship
15 The Chambers, Vineyard, Abingdon OX14 3FE
Tel: 01865 319700; Fax: 01865 319701
Email: enquiries@brf.org.uk
Website: www.brf.org.uk
BRF is a Registered Charity

ISBN 978 0 85746 390 6

Acknowledgements

The New Revised Standard Version of the Bible, Anglicized Edition, copyright © 1989, 1995 by the Division of Christian Education of the National Council of the Churches of Christ in the USA. Used by permission. All rights reserved.

Scripture quotations taken from The Holy Bible, New International Version (Anglicised edition) copyright © 1979, 1984, 2011 by Biblica. Used by permission of Hodder & Stoughton Publishers, an Hachette UK company. All rights reserved. 'NIV' is a registered trademark of Biblica. UK trademark number 1448790.

Extracts from the Authorised Version of the Bible (The King James Bible), the rights in which are vested in the Crown, are reproduced by permission of the Crown's Patentee, Cambridge University Press.

Extracts from CEB copyright © 2011 by Common English Bible.

Printed by Gutenberg Press, Tarxien, Malta

The Upper Room: how to use this book

The Upper Room is ideal in helping us spend a quiet time with God each day. Each daily entry is based on a passage of scripture, and is followed by a meditation and prayer. Each person who contributes a meditation to the magazine seeks to relate their experience of God in a way that will help those who use *The Upper Room* every day.

Here are some guidelines to help you make best use of *The Upper Room*:

1. Read the passage of Scripture. It is a good idea to read it more than once, in order to have a fuller understanding of what it is about and what you can learn from it.
2. Read the meditation. How does it relate to your own experience? Can you identify with what the writer has outlined from their own experience or understanding?
3. Pray the written prayer. Think about how you can use it to relate to people you know, or situations that need your prayers today.
4. Think about the contributor who has written the meditation. Some Upper Room users include this person in their prayers for the day.
5. Meditate on the 'Thought for the Day' and the 'Prayer Focus', perhaps using them again as the focus for prayer or direction for action.

Why is it important to have a daily quiet time? Many people will agree that it is the best way of keeping in touch every day with the God who sustains us, and who sends us out to do his will and show his love to the people we encounter each day. Meeting with God in this way reassures us of his presence with us, helps us to discern his will for us and makes us part of his worldwide family of Christian people through our prayers.

I hope that you will be encouraged as you use the magazine regularly as part of your daily devotions, and that God will richly bless you as you read his word and seek to learn more about him.

Susan Hibbins
UK Editor

In Times of/For Help with . . .

Below is a list of entries in this copy of *The Upper Room* relating to situations or emotions with which we may need help:

'Do not be anxious about anything, but in every situation, by prayer and petition, with thanksgiving, present your requests to God' (Philippians 4:6).

The work of *The Upper Room* has always been to lift individual voices into a worldwide communion of prayer, and an essential part of that ministry is our Living Prayer Centre. When this initiative was launched more than three decades ago, our volunteers responded to prayer requests via letters and phone calls, but evolving technology now allows us to connect through email and the internet.

In 2014 alone, we received a total of almost 275,000 requests from every medium. Of those, almost 40,000 were submitted to our website—and the power of the internet has been growing since October of that year, when we created a space for visitors to post their prayer requests publicly. We've been amazed that almost a third of the people making prayer requests allow them to be read by other visitors and many who read them are reaching out with their own responses.

Prayer is an essential practice of faith; it strengthens our connection to God. But we know that people also hunger for a sense that they do not pray alone. They hunger for a human connection and, incredibly, we're discovering that many people are able to receive this through the gift of technology.

As we begin 2016, we are mindful that the apostle Paul beckons us to present our requests to God 'in every situation'. Our challenge is to open new opportunities to do so. My hope is that we will find ways to draw those who pray into a community of love and support that not only responds to their urgent need but also places them in a daily walk with other brothers and sisters in the faith.

Sarah Wilke, Publisher

Rätt kurs, the Swedish edition of *The Upper Room*, began in 1950 with the support of the Methodist Church of Sweden. Throughout its long history, the Swedish edition has served readers in Sweden and Finland. Today *Rätt kurs* has a circulation of about 3000.

Rätt kurs and the people who translate and distribute the magazine also have a long history of serving those who are imprisoned in Sweden. Beginning in the 1960s, a number of churches and pastors began sharing *Rätt kurs* with prisoners as part of their ministry with prisons. This resource is still available to pastors and churches for use in prison ministries; local churches and pastors help pay for postage.

About a third of the copies printed for each issue of *Rätt kurs* are distributed in prisons throughout Sweden. As editors and distributors of *Rätt kurs*, we continue to have close relationships with the pastors who engage in prison ministry and view them as 'Rätt kurs ambassadors'. We believe that it is important for prisoners to be able to read in their own language so in addition to *Rätt kurs*, we distribute copies of several different language editions of *The Upper Room* including English, Spanish, Russian, Polish, Greek and Portuguese.

As you read this issue of *The Upper Room*, please pray for those who are able to connect with God through the pages of *Rätt kurs* and all of the other language editions of *The Upper Room*.

Bitte and Tomas Boström
Editors and Distributors of Rätt kurs
Swedish Edition of The Upper Room

The Editor writes...

On one of the roads along which I drive regularly on my way to our nearest market town there is a notice just underneath the 30 speed limit sign not far from the end of a village street. It says simply 'Keep going!' It is intended, I am sure, to draw attention to the fact that 30 is still the speed motorists should be observing.

I couldn't help but see it as a sign of encouragement in our spiritual lives instead. There are so many times when just to keep going is all we can manage. Sometimes our Christian lives seem to flow along easily: we rejoice in our relationship with Jesus; prayer and meditation on the Bible are a delight, and all that we try to do to serve God is successful.

If you are anything like me, however, there are also times when life is not at all easy. Life's events—difficult relationships, work problems, bereavement and family issues—affect everyone sooner or later. Even our church life does not always run smoothly and disagreements can occur there just as easily as anywhere else. Our devotional time may suffer because we are extra busy and distracted, and our prayers can become dry as dust.

What should we do when we feel like this? Sometimes we simply have to 'keep going'; difficult times do pass and problems are resolved. The most important thing I have discovered, though, is to hold fast to my routine of Bible reading and spending time with God. If I let this discipline slide, a lot more slides with it, and I find myself less able to cope with what life happens to be throwing at me.

It is amazing, too, that what we read in our devotional time is often exactly what we need to help us. It is no accident that we read something which speaks directly to the issue that is troubling us, showing us the power of scripture to go exactly where it is needed most.

I pray that in your daily reading you too will find what you need to 'keep going' each day.

Susan Hibbins
Editor of the UK edition

The Bible readings are selected with great care, and we urge you to include the suggested reading in your devotional time.

The Shrinking Garden

Read 1 Corinthians 2:4–13

When I was a child, I spoke like a child, I thought like a child, I reasoned like a child; when I became an adult, I put an end to childish ways.
1 Corinthians 13:11 (NRSV)

'When did this place shrink?' My grandfather laughed at my question as we stood in his back garden. I could remember where the swings, toys and basketball goal had once stood. As a child, I felt that this land of play was the widest in God's creation. Even the fence enclosing us once seemed taller than the trees.

Now there is only one porch swing and a small shed where we stored our bikes. The fence and I are the same height. Fifteen steps are enough to take me across the widest part of the lawn. I already knew the answer to my question before I asked it. The garden was the same size that it had always been. I was the one who had grown.

Our perspective changes as we grow up. As we learn to look at the world from God's perspective, 'big' problems become as small as that garden. Many things in the world do not change, but how we view the world can change. With God's help, we can seek to have the mind of Christ and see things from his point of view.

Prayer: *Loving God, open our hearts to change as we grow in our relationship with you. In Jesus' name we pray. Amen*

Thought for the day: Today I will try harder to see my world as God sees it.

Darian Duckworth (Mississippi, US)

Prayer Assignments

Read Philippians 4:4–9

Pray for one another... The prayer of the righteous is powerful and effective.

James 5:16 (NRSV)

When my polio flared up after 51 years, I was confined to bed with debilitating weakness. I felt helpless and utterly useless. 'What good is my life?' I thought, 'I can barely take care of myself, let alone help anyone else.' My husband reassured me, 'You probably haven't finished your work yet.'

One night I had a vivid dream: many children approached me, and I laid my hands on their heads, praying for each one. When I awoke I wondered, 'Is prayer the "work" I have yet to do? Who needs my prayers?'

The next day a TV reporter highlighted an amber alert for a child in Iowa. Then the late news showed photos of two children whose father had died in Iraq while serving in the US army. Each tragedy and need became my prayer assignment as I asked God to care for these children. During my three months of bed rest, prayer assignments changed my mood as well as my attitude. Prayer was the work I could do.

Prayer is a privilege God gives each of us to bless others. Besides enriching our lives and the lives of those for whom we pray, our prayers for others will someday bring our Master's commendation: 'Well done, good and faithful servant!' (Matthew 25:21, NIV).

Prayer: *Dear God, we trust you to work 'behind the scenes' as we pray. Help us to fulfil whatever work assignments you give us. Amen*

Thought for the day: Have I finished the work God has given me?

Helen Haidle (Oregon, US)

The First Step

Read Matthew 3:13–17

A voice from heaven said, 'This is my Son, the Beloved, with whom I am well pleased.'

Matthew 3:17 (NRSV)

I had read today's quoted verse, which appears straight after the baptism of Jesus in the Gospel of Matthew, perhaps hundreds of times. Yet when I read these words again recently, I was struck by a sudden insight: these words were spoken before Jesus began his earthly ministry.

I wondered what would cause this voice from heaven to say, 'This is my Son, the Beloved, with whom I am well pleased.' The teaching, the healing, the comfort for the afflicted, the affliction for those a little too comfortable, the words of hope, the wisdom of the sermon on the mount and the parables, and the cross and the resurrection—none of these had happened yet. The baptism of Jesus was only the first step in the great ministry which God had planned for him.

Jesus began his ministry and mission knowing that God was well pleased with him. I think God is already well pleased with us as we take the first step in any new ministry. This prompted me to ask myself, 'What first step do I need to take in order to begin whatever mission God has set aside for me?' We can trust that as we take that first step, God is already well pleased!

Prayer: *O God, as we step forth ready to serve in your name, challenge us and bless us. Amen*

Thought for the day: I want to hear God say, 'Beloved, I am well pleased with you.'

Frank Ramirez (Pennsylvania, US)

Not What I'd Planned

Read Romans 8:24–28
Cast all your anxiety on [God] because he cares for you.
1 Peter 5:7 (NIV)

A job I had once enjoyed had become very unpleasant. The atmosphere was full of tension, and I didn't know what to do about it. One morning I prayed, leaving the whole situation in God's hands. The next day, I lost my job. Obviously, this was not the solution I had anticipated, and I was concerned about finances. Even so, I felt a strange sense of peace, a sense that somehow this was the answer to my prayer. Whenever anxious thoughts returned, I would pray again, and the peace of God would calm my fears.

Through this experience, I learned to trust God. Eventually I was offered a much better job and found peace in knowing that God had been present through it all. Now when the worries of life come, I remember the time that God answered my prayer in a different way from what I had hoped for, and my peace returns.

God cares for each of us and will bring us what is best for us. We need only to pray and trust him and then act on his guidance.

Prayer: *Dear Lord, help us to release everything in our lives into your loving care. Amen*

Thought for the day: In all situations, God is working.

Tandy Balson (Alberta, Canada)

Dry and Weary Land

Read Psalm 42:1–8

I seek you, [my God], my soul thirsts for you; my flesh faints for you, as in a dry and weary land where there is no water.
Psalm 63:1 (NRSV)

Several years ago, my family and I moved to New Mexico. Living in a desert has given me a new understanding of the Bible's references to a dry and weary land. Here, it seems as if nothing grows except near a stream or river. Near the river beautiful farmland flourishes and flowering trees bloom for most of the season. But even half a mile from the water, nearly everything dries up.

Just as plants draw nourishment from water, we find the nourishment we need to grow spiritually in time spent with God. What happens when we neglect to spend time with him? At first we may thirst, but if we ignore it, this awareness of our thirst will eventually fade. Just like water in a desert when it is cut off from its source, our relationship with God will dry up.

But we can flourish in our Christian life when we acknowledge that Jesus Christ is the water of life and when we receive strength from him. Jesus said to the Samaritan woman at the well, 'The water that I will give will become in them a spring of water gushing up to eternal life' (John 4:14). Staying connected to God's living water requires work. Disciplines such as spending time with him in prayer, studying the Bible and learning how to listen for God's voice are all part of growing in our relationship with Christ. When we seek God every day, we can be sure that our thirst will be quenched by living water.

Prayer: *Dear God, fill us with your living water today so we can walk in your love. Amen*

Thought for the day: How am I seeking God today?

Ken Edwards (New Mexico, US)

An Eye-Opening Experience

Read Matthew 20:29–34

[Two blind men] say unto [Jesus], 'Lord, that our eyes may be opened.'
Matthew 20:33 (KJV)

'I don't like retirement. I feel I have no purpose,' I complained to God. I couldn't get out of the rut I seemed to be in that day.

Later that afternoon I took a walk with my two-year-old great-nephew. He wasn't satisfied to just walk; he wanted to explore the world beyond the road. We watched a robin pull a juicy worm from a newly mown lawn, we waved and smiled at an elderly neighbour, we paused to feel the wind in our hair and chased our shadows in the sunshine. My attitude changed. I was no longer focused on my worries; my eyes had opened to the world around me.

In our reading for today, Jesus changed the perspective of two blind men who probably felt that their lives were going nowhere. Jesus' presence and compassion gave their world a new perspective when he opened their eyes. Now they could look into the eyes of loved ones and enjoy the beauty around them. Not only did they receive physical vision, but they gained new spiritual vision that day.

We all get discouraged some days, but it's important to remember that Jesus also crosses our path each day. If we ask him, he will open our eyes to the hope offered for each one of us.

Prayer: *Dear Lord, give us eyes to see beyond our limited vision. Teach us to see you in our everyday lives. Amen*

Thought for the day: I will watch for Jesus to pass my way today.

Connie L. Coppings (Kentucky, US)

Playing For God

Read Matthew 25:14–29

I can do all things through [Christ] who strengthens me.
Philippians 4:13 (NRSV)

When I was in Australia completing my bachelor's degree, I attended a small church that did not have enough pianists. I felt God calling me to play the piano for this church. But I hesitated, wondering if I was skilled enough to do so. I had never had any serious piano lessons or any other training for this role. As a result, I felt anxious and worried.

Just as I was about to turn away from God's nudging, I heard one of the preachers quote in his sermon the above verse from Philippians. He encouraged us to act on our callings and persevere to develop the talents God has given us. No matter how small our talent, if we have faith and are willing to work hard and keep using our talent, God will use it for the kingdom.

Now I have been playing in church services for a few years. I still have some way to go to improve my skills, but I never regret that I took that first step and let God work through me.

Prayer: *Merciful Father, thank you for your love and for the opportunity to serve you. Help us to use our talents for the glory of your name. Amen*

Thought for the day: God is able to grow even my smallest seed of talent into something glorious.

Silvia Lokajaya (Jakarta, Indonesia)

Our Youthful God

Read Psalm 71:9–18
We do not lose heart. Though outwardly we are wasting away, yet inwardly we are being renewed day by day.
2 Corinthians 4:16 (NIV)

At times the challenges of ageing—aches and pains, strained eyesight, muffled hearing, and 'senior moments'—cause doubts and fears within me. Troubling questions surface. Will my mind fall prey to dementia? Will I lose mobility and have to go into care? Will unforeseen circumstances deplete my finances? Sometimes I even imagine that God is growing feeble within me.

When my faith is challenged by these questions, I recall what God has done in the past. He lifted my family out of a financial crisis and sustained us during my back surgery. He helped me to overcome the rejection and ridicule of others when I faced a personal trial. When I reflect on my life, I realise that God has never failed me.

Recalling these instances reminds me that God's power has not waned. While the strength and vigour of my physical body fade, the eternal youth of God's Holy Spirit restores my soul daily. I am constantly assured that God, who empowered and guided me throughout my working years, is also able to help me meet the demands of ageing.

Prayer: *Dear God, thank you for being with us and sustaining us throughout the challenges of each stage of life. Amen*

Thought for the day: Even as I grow older, God restores my soul daily.

Steven Thompson (Iowa, US)

Shine On

Read John 1:1–9

God made two great lights—the greater light to govern the day and the lesser light to govern the night.
Genesis 1:16 (NIV)

Recently, the moon was closer to the Earth than it would be at any other time during the year. Because of its nearness, the moon appeared larger and brighter than usual. The brilliant light shone by the 'super-moon' cast shadows in my garden just as the sun does during the day. The moon seemed to produce its own glow; however, its luminescence was but a reflection of the sun's intense radiance.

I want to be like that super-moon at all times, brilliantly reflecting a power greater than my own. I ask myself: 'Do I regularly display kindness, forgiveness and love? Am I a good example for others to follow? Or do I shine brightly only on rare occasions? Do I perform good deeds so that others will praise me or because I know that doing so is God's will for me?' When I consciously draw nearer to God my thoughts, words and actions can more intensely reflect his love to others.

Prayer: *God of the universe, thank you for the wonders of creation that display your almighty power and glory. Help us to be true reflections of you to others. Amen*

Thought for the day: Today I will be a light that reflects God's love.

Lu Fullilove (Texas, US)

PRAYER FOCUS: THOSE WHO WORK NIGHT SHIFTS

Finding Purpose

Read Proverbs 31:10–31

She is vigilant over the activities of her household; she doesn't eat the food of laziness. Her children bless her; her husband praises her.
Proverbs 31:27–28 (CEB)

For a long time, I felt that I had little or no value because I was a stay-at-home mum. Not being in the workforce or helping to earn a living for the family took a toll on me. I thought that if I couldn't contribute a wage, what could I give to my family? I became increasingly stressed to the point of giving up. I felt like a nobody.

In those moments of despair, I felt God speak gently to my heart. Through prayer, scripture and other reading he helped me to step back from my negative thoughts and to look around me. I began to see that my calling was in the lives of my little girls, giggling with joy as they showed me their latest fashion creations. It was in the calm gratitude my husband displayed at having a hot, home-cooked meal prepared for the family to eat after a long day. It was in working in the garden and with the livestock on our farm to provide healthy food to eat, and in teaching my family about the love of God.

My sense of self-worth is no longer tied to earning a wage; instead I want to be the best wife and mother I can be, whether or not I contribute to the household income. Now I know who I am, and I know that what I do matters.

Prayer: *Loving Lord, help us to seek you first. Give us patience and strength to follow your calling. Amen*

Thought for the day: My self-worth rests not in a weekly pay cheque but in God's love for me.

Samantha Parsons (West Virginia, US)

Needing a Refuge?

Read Psalm 91:1–4

You are my fortress, my refuge in times of trouble.
Psalm 59:16 (NIV)

Earlier this morning, on a cold and stormy day, I set out for town and got soaked. What a relief to reach the first shop and hurry through the door! It was a haven of light and warmth. Two other people were heading in the same direction so we all bundled through the door together.

It was so good to enjoy that sheltering place. Now, home and dry again, I've been thinking of other sheltering places I've valued down the years—such as a cool shady tree on a blistering hot day, or a convenient rock to protect me from a high wind, to say nothing of my old umbrella beneath which I've huddled through many a deluge.

There have been a number of times when I've needed God's kindly and strong protection too. When you're up against it, God's presence is a good place to go to. The Bible mentions storms and sheltering places so often because God wants us to always find a refuge in him.

Prayer: *Lord, thank you that you are a safe shelter for us. May we be quick to turn to you when we find ourselves in the middle of a storm. Amen*

Thought for the day: My refuge is my God, the God who loves me.

Elaine Brown (Perthshire, Scotland)

Eyes to See

Read Luke 7:36–50

Jesus turned to the woman and said to Simon, 'Do you see this woman?'
Luke 7:44 (CEB)

When I was a student, a member of the faculty made me aware that he knew who I was and that he cared about my ability to understand his lectures. One day when he was introducing a new subject, I must have looked confused. The professor stopped, looked straight at me, and said, 'You don't get it, do you, Dickson?' His comment could have been embarrassing, but he seemed to see that I was lost and needed help to understand the subject.

Jesus said to Simon, the Pharisee, 'Do you see this woman?' Simon saw only a sinful person who did not belong at his dinner party; and he assumed that Jesus was a bit dull not to perceive that she was to be ignored.

Often we have eyes that do not see. The story in today's reading calls us all to see people with whom we interact each day not as stereotypes but as real people with needs, gifts and great possibilities—for that is the way God sees us all. The biblical message is that God—who came in Jesus Christ—sees us, knows us, died for us and cares for us. Our lives can be made new when we respond to God's redeeming love as our Saviour and Lord.

Prayer: *Dear God, give us eyes to see the people around us and hearts to care for them as Christ has loved us. Amen*

Thought for the day: I will look for God in everyone I see today.

Elmer Dickson (Florida, US)

Not Alone

Read John 14:15–20

I will not leave you as orphans; I will come to you.
John 14:18 (NIV)

Sending postcards from holidays abroad is not as popular as it once was, but it is always a pleasure to receive cards from friends and to know, wherever they are, that they arrived safely and are well.

'Ring or text me when you get there,' is a common request when a friend leaves us after a visit, or when a son or daughter is travelling alone. We need to know that all is well with their lives when they leave us; we miss them when they have left.

Jesus left his companions when he ascended to heaven. The Bible tells us that they returned to Jerusalem with great joy because they believed his promises (Luke 24:50–53), though they must have missed the physical presence of their friend and Lord.

Jesus didn't promise to ring or send a postcard. Instead he promised to send them a Comforter, a guide and an inner strength in the person of the Holy Spirit: 'I will ask the Father, and he will give you another advocate to help you and be with you for ever—the Spirit of truth' (John 14:16). They had to wait a little while, but what joy they experienced when the Holy Spirit came to them (Acts 2:1–11). Then they knew that what Jesus had said—'On that day you will realise that I am in my Father, and you are in me, and I am in you'—was true, that he was now with his Father and that they would never be alone. And neither will we.

Prayer: *Loving Lord, thank you for sending the Holy Spirit to be our Comforter and guide. Help us to be aware of the Spirit's guidance each day. Amen*

Thought for the day: The Holy Spirit is with me today.

Iris Lloyd (Berkshire, England)

PRAYER FOCUS: FAMILY MEMBERS WHO ARE TRAVELLING TODAY

Becoming a Better Disciple

Read James 1:17–26
Be doers of the word, and not merely hearers who deceive themselves.
James 1:22 (NRSV)

When I began regularly attending church, I rarely missed a service, Bible study or special event. Despite all the time I spent hearing God's word and Jesus' teachings, the message did not grow in me in the way it was intended. Instead of becoming more Christ-like, I often used my new-found religion to judge others for missing church or not meeting my moral code. I believed the only way to God was by having your body in the church building. Needless to say, my attitude had a negative effect on others.

My best friend helped me change my mind by telling me I had completely turned Jesus' teaching upside down with my pious attitude. Though I was angry with him at first, it finally hit me that he was right. Instead of showing love, speaking peace and making disciples with the words of Jesus, I was driving people away with my false sense of morality.

After realising this, I tried to learn from my mistakes. I reread my Bible and adjusted my attitudes and actions. I still attend my church regularly, but I have learned that disciples are shaped by what they are taught, not by where they are taught. God works through others to remind us of the standards Jesus set for us.

Prayer: *Dear Lord, help us to judge others less and love them more. Amen*

Thought for the day: Today I will be a doer of God's word.

Mark Carter (Texas, US)

Wherever We Go

Read Joshua 1:1–9

Be strong and courageous; do not be frightened or dismayed, for the Lord your God is with you wherever you go.
Joshua 1:9 (NRSV)

I was visiting a missionary friend in Mexico City. We had spent the day exploring its many beautiful and interesting sites. We were on the subway, travelling home at the end of the day when suddenly the city was hit by a small earthquake. We were plunged into darkness as the power failed and the train coasted to a stop between stations.

The change in the crowded car was instant and dramatic. Where just moments before I had been chatting happily, anticipating a good meal and more time spent visiting friends, I was suddenly faced with the terrifying knowledge that I was trapped far below the streets. As I felt panic beginning to rise in me, through the darkness I felt my friend take my hand. Her touch reminded me that I was not alone, and I was immediately comforted as we waited for the situation to be resolved.

The Bible promises us that we have the Lord's comforting presence with us wherever we go. God delights to hold our hand in the dark places of life, where we feel alone, forgotten and afraid. Remembering this, we can find the help and comfort we need to return to the light.

Prayer: *Take our hand, God, today and every day. Remind us that because of your love, we are never alone. Amen*

Thought for the day: No matter how deep the darkness, God will bring light.

Devonna R. Allison (Michigan, US)

A Good Taste in a Sour World

Read Psalm 34:1–22
Taste and see that the Lord is good.
Psalm 34:8 (NIV)

My family and I have been working with the poor in Northern Bangladesh for five years. During this time we have endured and witnessed many hardships. One night, I despaired when a friend came to us in tears after storms had destroyed her roof, exposing her family to the harsh monsoon rains. As if that were not enough, the deluge was starting to wash away her clay house. She had no savings for repairs because thieves had broken into her house a few days earlier. We both felt as if everything was stacked against her.

Though we could not repair her roof, my wife and I read Psalm 34 with her to remind us that God is good and to hold on to the promise, as the psalmist did, as we wait to be delivered from our fears (v. 4). Our friend left us, encouraged. Later we heard that her house was saved when a close friend was able to install a new roof before the house completely washed away.

The psalmist challenges us to seek the Lord and to keep praising God, even in the midst of trouble. The promise is that we will see God's goodness and it will be so good that we can truly taste it.

Prayer: *Dear Lord, thank you for being our safe refuge and for hearing us when we cry out to you. Help us to seek your righteousness more each day. Amen*

Thought for the day: In difficult times, I can take refuge in God.

David Powell (Bangladesh)

Freely Given

Read James 2:14–26

For by grace you have been saved through faith, and this is not your own doing; it is the gift of God—not the result of works.
Ephesians 2:8–9 (NRSV)

My father wanted to give me an extravagant gift for my 40th birthday. I was embarrassed that he wanted to spend so much money. He replied, 'You do so much for me. I want to thank you for what you do.' I told him that I help him not to be paid back but because I love him and want to help.

As I said those words I realised that for many years I had been confused by what seemed to be conflicting directives in scripture: some passages tell us to do good works (see James 2:14–16), and others tell us that our good works are worthless (see Galatians 2:16). But now, thanks to my father's gift, I understand. I love my father so I help him; my father loves me so he gives me a gift. Neither depends on the other. I do good deeds to show my love, not because I am promised something in return.

Both my earthly and heavenly fathers appreciate my actions because in them they see my love for them. They give me gifts not to pay me for what I do, but because I am their child. Each action strengthens the other, but neither requires the other. Thus, we receive eternal life because we are God's children through faith in Christ. We do good works because we appreciate all that God has given to us and want others to be blessed as we are.

Prayer: *Dear God, thank you for your gift of eternal life, a gift that you alone bestow. In Jesus' name we pray. Amen*

Thought for the day: How have I shown my love for God today?

Dawn M. Adams (Massachusetts, US)

Remember to Breathe

Read Matthew 6:25–34
Jesus said, 'Come unto me, all ye that labour and are heavy laden, and I will give you rest.'
Matthew 11:28 (KJV)

I recently went to the local hospital, where I had a painful medical procedure. At one point, the doctor stopped what he was doing and told me to breathe. I didn't realise that pain had caused me to hold my breath, but several times throughout the procedure the doctor stopped and reminded me to breathe again.

A few days later, I realised that I have lived my life in the same way. Every time a problem or an unexpected challenge came along, I held my breath through it. I became stressed and could not relax. I knew that God had shown me mercy by helping me through difficult times. I also realised that he didn't want me to hold my breath throughout my life. God wanted me to rest in faith, knowing that no matter what problem I was facing, he would help me through it.

I'm never alone; and even if another person does not remind me to breathe, God is always with me assuring me that I can rest. Knowing this, I can relax and breathe in his presence.

Prayer: *Breathing in, say: 'Loving God.'*
Breathing out, say: 'You are with us in all our troubles.'
Amen

Thought for the day: God is our constant companion and helper.

Shirley Rose (Illinois, US)

Criticism

Read 2 Corinthians 7:2–11
If I caused you sorrow by my letter, I do not regret it… because your sorrow led you to repentance.
2 Corinthians 7:8–9 (NIV)

I was devastated to see red marks and scribbled messages on every page of the first report I had written in my new job. I thought the report represented my best work, but my boss did not agree.

We have all been criticised. Unfortunately, it is rarely a pleasant experience. However, when properly delivered, even criticism can be beneficial and productive.

The Apostle Paul had detractors who criticised him to the church at Corinth. They claimed Paul was uncaring, untrustworthy and unqualified. As a result, Paul defended his ministry. He tells us in today's reading that he realised his words hurt his audience. Although we tend to discourage actions that cause others discomfort, Paul affirms that criticism can sometimes be necessary. However, we must realise that the purpose of it is not to hurt people but to result in correction and growth.

Paul said he was happy and didn't regret his words because of their ultimate result. Understanding Paul's words helped me to understand the criticism I had received and to use it to rewrite the report to make it better. Criticism well offered and received can glorify God.

Prayer: *Dear Father, give us wisdom to accept constructive criticism in the spirit in which it is given and compassion to offer the same with a gracious spirit. Amen*

Thought for the day: Gracious criticism can help us grow in our work and faith.

Dan Boutwell (Texas, US)

Compassion in Action

Read Nehemiah 5:1–12

Faith by itself, if it has no works, is dead.
James 2:17 (NRSV)

When I was at school, I witnessed an act of compassion I will never forget. A boy using crutches fell in the entrance to our school. I watched with dismay and did not know what to do. Meanwhile, Diana, another student, asked him if he needed help. When he responded yes, she came to his aid. She allowed her feeling of compassion to become an act of compassion.

In our scripture reading for today, we see that Nehemiah was also filled with compassion and acted accordingly. The Israelites were complaining that they lacked food, and were forced to mortgage their fields and borrow money at huge interest rates. They also had to sell their children as slaves. They suffered these things at the hands of fellow Israelites, not foreigners. Nehemiah confronted the guilty ones and got them to change their ways.

Nehemiah showed leadership not just by empathising but also by doing something to improve the situation. He didn't just feel the pain of others; he was moved to help them. As God's servants we too are called to respond with mercy and to put his love into action.

Prayer: *Dear God of compassion, help us to go beyond just feeling and become doers of your word and work. Amen*

Thought for the day: I am a hearer of God's word; I can also be a doer (see James 1:22).

Lin Daniels (Massachusetts, US)

Hard Work, Low Pay...

Read Genesis 31:38–42

We also glory in our sufferings, because we know that suffering produces perseverance; perseverance, character; and character, hope.
Romans 5:3–4 (NIV)

As a young man, looking for adventure in the outdoors and not knowing what else to do with my life, I joined the California Conservation Corps. Their recruiting motto is 'Hard work, low pay, miserable conditions... and more!' The thrill of my new adventure was soon tempered by the fact that the motto was true. I was working hard for low wages in a difficult environment.

As a new believer in Christ, I was beginning to discover the connection between my perseverance and God's desire to shape my character. Later, I read the biblical account of the way Laban tricked Jacob into working for a wife he did not choose. Under Laban's supervision, Jacob worked through extreme temperatures, sleepless nights and unfair treatment. And God blessed him because of his faithful endurance; he used the experience to shape Jacob's character.

The story is a reminder of how God can shape us through adversity. As we remain faithful and persevere through difficult circumstances, God is faithful to cultivate in us the character of Christ. By God's grace, we can emerge from our trials stronger and more conformed to the image of Christ.

Prayer: *Dear Lord, give us grace to endure adversity, confident that you are at work in us, making us more like Christ. Amen*

Thought for the day: Faithful endurance produces godly character.

Timothy Austin (Istanbul, Turkey)

My Daily Bread

Read Exodus 20:1–17

You shall not covet your neighbour's house; you shall not covet your neighbour's wife, or male or female slave, or ox, or donkey, or anything that belongs to your neighbour.

Exodus 20:17 (NRSV)

One day I stopped to feed some ducks on the canal that runs near my neighbourhood. Before long, a couple of ducks began fighting over a single piece of bread. One duck had pinned the other against the side of a bridge and was aggressively trying to peck his beak open to get the bread from him. I threw more bread in their direction, even landing some directly on their backs, but they were so focused on their fight over one piece that they didn't even notice the bread raining down upon them. Even after the first piece was gone, they dragged their fight into the water.

This reminded me of the commandment, 'Thou shalt not covet' (Exodus 20:17, KJV). It is difficult not to envy someone who has an exciting job, a beautiful house or a seemingly perfect family. But when we focus our attention on resenting or wanting what someone else has, we may fail to notice the ways God blesses us and provides for us daily. Jesus taught us to pray, 'Give us this day our daily bread', a statement of faith and expectation that God will provide us with what we need every day. Rather than comparing our lives to our neighbours', we can trust in God and open our hearts to eternal blessings.

Prayer: *Dear God, help us to open our hearts and minds to receive our daily bread. Amen*

Thought for the day: Today, I will give thanks for the blessings God has given me.

Susan Pospisil (Arkansas, US)

Even a Sigh

Read Psalm 139:1–10

You discern my going out and my lying down; you are familiar with all my ways.
Psalm 139:3 (NIV)

Until my battle with cancer I never understood the difference between being tired and being fatigued. When I was tired an inner push still allowed me to accomplish certain tasks. But when I was fatigued, I could push no more. I felt lower than a pothole. Sometimes I had no energy to eat, let alone take a shower. One morning I was so exhausted all I could do was sigh. Then in my devotions I discovered Psalm 38:9 (NRSV): 'O Lord, all my longing is known to you; my sighing is not hidden from you.' What a boost I felt in my spirit! God understood my deepest sigh, no matter how low or weak I felt. God loved me no matter how weary or discouraged I had become. He knew how I felt and what I longed for.

I am overwhelmed by God's intimate love for us—that he listens for something as small as a sigh. Though our suffering may seem a huge burden, it can never keep God from caring for us.

Prayer: *Dear God, we thank you that there is nothing—no matter how disabling—that can keep us from you. In our suffering be our comforter and bring us peace. Amen*

Thought for the day: No matter how low I feel, God offers grace to lift me up.

Mark Weinrich (Nevada, US)

Offering Buckets

Read Psalm 136:1–3

O give thanks to the God of heaven, for his steadfast love endures for ever.

Psalm 136:26 (NRSV)

The children's message that Sunday was about the psalmist's confidence that 'God's steadfast love endures for ever'. The person giving the message took bright yellow plastic beach buckets and pantomimed pouring out God's love on to the children. When she 'emptied' one bucket, she would bring out another one. Just as the psalmist repeats the phrase, 'his steadfast love endures for ever' several times, she used several buckets to make sure the children understood that God's love never runs out. There's always another 'bucketful'.

Later in the service, when it was time to take up the offering, the minister got those buckets out again and said, 'Since God's love is unending, our offerings to God should be, too. We are going to take up the offering in these buckets today and return to God our thanks in response to his steadfast love for us.'

No matter how big our offering plates or buckets are, we can never repay God for pouring out enduring love for us. But when we give back to God with thankful hearts, we are responding to that love in ways that further his reign on earth. Remembering how blessed and loved we are, we, in turn, can show God's love by giving 'bucketsful' of love to his people every day.

Prayer: *Lord of love, help us to become more loving toward others in the world you have created for us all. Amen*

Thought for the day: How much love can I give to others today?

Xavia Arndt Sheffield (Maryland, US)

The Little Things

Read 2 Corinthians 9:7–15

Whenever we have an opportunity, let us work for the good of all, and especially for those of the family of faith.

Galatians 6:10 (NRSV)

We were leisurely playing a game when the phone rang and one of my daughters ran to answer it. We have taught her to answer the phone with 'good morning' or 'good evening' followed by 'God bless you.' The caller did not reply, but we could hear her sobbing softly. My daughter was a bit startled and called me to the phone. It was a good friend of ours and when she regained her composure she said: 'I apologise. It's just that it's been a while since someone has said "God bless you" to me. When I heard your daughter's voice, I truly felt God saying those words to me.'

We can do so much to share God's love through the little things. People need to feel and experience God's love. They need someone to show concern, to listen or perhaps to share a gentle embrace. Today, tomorrow or on any given day, God can use each of us to bless someone.

Prayer *Creator God, help us to be caring, useful people who are blessings to others. In the name of Jesus. Amen*

Thought for the day: Even little things bear witness to the love of God.

Reninaldo Santana-Rabell (Vega Alta, Puerto Rico)

Trained Eyes

Read Luke 24:13–32

Their eyes were opened and they recognised [Jesus].
Luke 24:31 (NIV)

I shield my eyes from the afternoon sun and peer up into the huge tree in our garden. An owl has taken up residence there. Each day I look expectantly, hoping to spot our new neighbour, perched high in his new abode. Unfortunately, this feathered friend is difficult to see, unless you are my husband, who has a trained eye.

When I look and look and can't seem to locate the owl, I become discouraged, convinced he has moved on to a new habitat. However, my husband can peer through the foliage to see what I cannot. He assures me, 'Yes, he's still here.' Then he points and patiently directs my gaze.

We can train our eyes to spot God as well. As we recall God's faithfulness in our lives, we develop eyes of faith—eyes that will see his presence, regardless of the circumstances. When those around us have lost sight of God, it is our privilege and responsibility to reassure them, 'Yes, my friend, God is still here.' Then, with words of faith, we can point them toward God, guiding them to see and discover him in the midst of their situation.

Prayer: *Faithful God, you have promised to never leave us. Give us opportunities to use our eyes of faith to reassure those around us of your faithful presence in their lives. In Jesus' name. Amen*

Thought for the day: Today I will look for opportunities to point others to God's presence.

Stacy Sanchez (New Mexico, US)

Praying Out Loud

Read Romans 8:35–39

Neither death, nor life… nor things present, nor things to come, nor powers, nor height, nor depth, nor anything else in all creation, will be able to separate us from the love of God.

Romans 8:38–39 (NRSV)

As someone who struggles with anxiety, I find the verse quoted above extremely comforting. Fear and worry are not just things I can turn off with the flick of a switch; they are always lurking in the back of my mind, waiting for the chance to consume me.

In particular I fear praying aloud in public. My heart races; I can't concentrate or find the words to speak. Then I give in to my fear and ask someone else to pray.

I know that by surrendering to this fear I'm missing the opportunity to connect with the Holy Spirit and to allow God's Spirit to bless me and those with whom I might pray.

I often give in to my fears because it is less scary in the short term. Facing my fears takes unbelievable strength. I have learned that if I am to overcome my fears, I will have to ask God for help and then be willing to accept that help in whatever form it comes.

Neither today's fears nor worries about tomorrow can separate us from God's love. Knowing this, we can find comfort that even when we are afraid, we have the promise of God's unrelenting love.

Prayer: *Dear Father, we thank you for your love and strength that help us overcome fears that threaten to overwhelm us. Amen*

Thought for the day: When worry and fear threaten me, I will remember God's love.

Kelly Howard (Georgia, US)

Love in Action

Read Matthew 7:7–12

In everything, do to others what you would have them do to you, for this sums up the Law and the Prophets.
Matthew 7:12 (NIV)

In the gym I belong to, each member has an electronic key to open the entry door. One cold day, I heard a tapping on the door's window but ignored the sound. The tapping stopped but then began again.

I glanced over my shoulder through the windowed entrance to see a young woman wearing lightweight exercise clothes and shivering from the cold. When I caught the eye of John, a fellow member, I asked, 'Do you know that lady?' He replied that he didn't but then hurried to open the door. The woman had forgotten her keys when she left the gym earlier and couldn't get into her car or back inside the building.

John had immediately responded to the woman's need—treating the shivering woman as a member, a part of the family. That's the way Christ would have us treat others. He calls us to open the door and welcome them with acceptance and hope. Christ understands each person's situation and asks us to respond to that person with love and respect. In this way, we can put God's love into action and enhance our relationships with others and with God.

Prayer: *Dear Lord, help us to listen and to look for opportunities to treat others the way we wish to be treated. Amen*

Thought for the day: Small kindnesses can show God's love in a practical way.

Aaron M. Zook, Jr (Texas, US)

Doing Good—Regardless

Read Philippians 1:1–6

Let us not become weary in doing good, for at the proper time we will reap a harvest if we do not give up.
Galatians 6:9 (NIV)

Years ago, I met a single mother who cleaned houses for a living. I hired her to clean mine to help her pay her bills. Then one day she stopped coming. I soon realised that she had stolen some of my property. My intentions for her were good, but I was hurt as a result.

After experiences like this, I sometimes hesitate to continue doing good. But when my will to do good becomes weak, I've learned that I need to pause—maybe for moments, maybe for days—and nurture my relationship with Christ. I whisper or sing words of thanksgiving. I thank him for giving me a confident hope of living in heaven, which puts life in perspective and helps me to endure my own trials. Then, I return to the fray of life and serve Christ with a refreshed spirit, looking forward to the harvest of blessing he will bring.

It's easy to feel discouraged when good intentions result in pain. But it helps to pause and thank Jesus for his promise to complete his work in the lives of all those who follow him (see Philippians 1:4–6). With this promise in mind, we can persevere in doing good for others—as Jesus has commanded.

Prayer: *Dear Jesus, may your promise to complete the work you've begun encourage us to persevere in doing good. Amen*

Thought for the day: When I'm weary of doing good, I will thank Jesus for the good he accomplishes through me.

Carol Wilson (Washington, US)

Sharing Joys and Sorrows

Read 1 Corinthians 9:19–23

Rejoice with those who rejoice, weep with those who weep.
Romans 12:15 (NRSV)

Last year, one of my friends experienced a devastating sorrow. All I could offer was empathy and prayer. While praying, I felt my heart filling with grief. I believe that when we are capable of crying with other people over their sorrows, we share in their suffering.

That same day, I needed to offer birthday wishes to another person. I wanted my words to be joyful and sincere. But for me this was inconceivable. I felt as if the dreary weather of winter was reigning in one courtyard and the full heat of summer in another.

I decided to pray before calling with my birthday greetings. To my surprise, I was able to share my friend's joy sincerely.

The power of God is revealed in surprising ways. He enables us to feel in our hearts that which we cannot even imagine in our minds.

Prayer: *Dear Lord, let us be empty vessels for those whose sorrow is overflowing, and fill us with compassion for those who are thirsting, as we pray, 'Our Father which art in heaven, Hallowed be thy name. Thy kingdom come. Thy will be done, as in heaven, so in earth. Give us day by day our daily bread. And forgive us our sins; for we also forgive every one that is indebted to us. And lead us not into temptation; but deliver us from evil.'* Amen*

Thought for the day: God enables us to both weep and rejoice with others.

Fedor Kim (Moscow, Russia)

PRAYER FOCUS: A FRIEND EXPERIENCING GREAT SORROW

* Luke 11:2–4 (KJV)

Hearing Aids

Read Matthew 13:9–17
Whoever has ears, let them hear.
Matthew 13:9 (NIV)

I began to lose my hearing in my thirties. I ignored it as long as I could. But when it began to interfere with my conversations with family and friends and at work, I knew I needed to do something. I have a degenerative condition and have had six ear surgeries over four years. I have limited hearing in my right ear and minimal hearing in my left ear. I now rely on hearing aids.

I discovered I had been missing out on so much when I was unable to hear fully. I was often frustrated and impatient, and I lacked calm and peace. The same results can occur in my relationship with God. When I don't spend time listening to and hearing what he has to say, I lose the fruit of the Spirit and my life lacks calm and peace. It is wonderful that God communicates in many different ways: through nature, through other people, and through the Bible.

I am so grateful that my hearing impairment does not interfere with my ability to connect with God.

Prayer: *Giver of all things, thank you that we don't need perfect hearing to hear you speak to us. Open our lives to the different ways we can know you. In Jesus' name. Amen*

Thought for the day: How can I hear God speaking to me today?

Tara Otis (Nebraska, US)

The Father's Son

Read John 14:1–14

Jesus replied, 'Don't you know me, Philip, even after I have been with you all this time? Whoever has seen me has seen the Father.'
John 14:9 (CEB)

As my husband and I were eating at a local restaurant I noticed that a young man entering the dining room seemed familiar. His actions and gestures led me to conclude that he was the son of one of our friends. Although I hadn't seen this young man since he was a child, I was able to identify him. His mannerisms, the way he walked and stood, were so much like his dad's that his identity was unmistakable.

The next day when thinking about how alike those two men were, another father/son relationship that reveals many similarities occurred to me. By observing Jesus and his interactions with others, we know much about God. Jesus always taught love. He was quick to forgive and he healed others. He was gentle, kind and compassionate. He assured us that there was nothing to fear. Since he is God's Son, we know that God has these same characteristics: loving, forgiving, gentle, kind and compassionate. We know God because we know Jesus.

Prayer: *Creator God, help us to be mindful of who we are, to act with love for others and to become more like Christ each day. Amen*

Thought for the day: I can reflect my heavenly Father's love in my words and actions.

Janet Holloway-Bergman (Missouri, US)

Bearing Fruit

Read Psalm 1:1–6

We are what [God] has made us, created in Christ Jesus for good works, which God prepared beforehand to be our way of life.
Ephesians 2:10 (NRSV)

The trees and bushes in my garden are a source of pleasure and wonder. In the beauty of their colourful blossoms and the taste of their fruit, I see God's marvellous work. A few years ago I planted an elderberry bush. These bushes have little white flowers clustered on the end of each stem like a puff of lace. The flowers give way to dark purple berries that I have discovered make a lovely jelly.

Fruit-bearing trees and bushes are a gift that inspires me. Just as God designed these plants to produce fruit, God calls me to bear fruit. He has a purpose for my life. As I mature in my relationship with God by studying the Bible, praying and working in community with other Christians, I discover and fulfil that purpose.

Our reading for today encourages us to root our faith in God's word. Then we will be like trees planted by streams of water that yield their fruit in season (v. 3). When we read God's word, believe it and obey it, we produce fruit and bring glory to God.

Prayer: *Thank you, Lord, for creating us with purpose. Help us to sink our roots deep into the soil of your goodness. Amen*

Thought for the day: We glorify God when we bear the fruit we are created to bring into the world.

Carol Van Der Woude (Illinois, US)

Bedside Prayer

Read Matthew 6:5–8

My soul is satisfied as with a rich feast, and my mouth praises you with joyful lips when I think of you.
Psalm 63:5–6 (NRSV)

At the age of 80 my mother became bedridden and moved to a care home. She remained there for five years and never complained.

When the priest from a local church visited, he came to my mother's room and offered to pray for her. My mother told him that she belonged to another denomination but saw no reason why he could not pray for her. When the priest had finished, my mother offered a prayer as well.

The following week, the priest visited her again. This time a young assistant accompanied him. The priest brought him to my mother's bedside and said to him: 'I want you to hear how this lady prays. It is as if she is conversing with God as a friend.'

God hears—and responds to—all our prayers. He wants us to feel a sense of closeness, like talking with a good friend who is sitting next to us or by our bedside. When we pray, we can share with God our everyday lives, knowing that he is ready to listen.

Prayer: *Loving God, thank you that when our strength fails and we are not able to serve you as before, we can still converse with you in prayer. Amen*

Thought for the day: Praying can be like visiting our best friend.

Arnoldo Canclini (Buenos Aires, Argentina)*

*Mr Canclini died while this issue was in production.

Gratitude for Answered Prayer

Read Romans 12:11–13

Do not be anxious about anything, but in every situation, by prayer and petition, with thanksgiving, present your requests to God.
Philippians 4:6 (NIV)

Recently, I have been praying daily for the big battles that I face. It occurred to me, however, that when my prayers are answered, I am not so steadfast in giving thanks as I am in my asking. I may thank God once or twice and move on to some other petition for others or for myself. I rarely recognise answers to prayers for the little things in my life.

Daily activities and troubles seem to guide my prayer life, and I love to pray for things such as restoration of a sickly flower I planted, or that God will heal my sick cat. Since God created all things, I pray for them, but I often fail to notice the answers to such prayers. When I do recognise these answered prayers, joy comes to my heart as I watch the sickly flower come alive and adjust to its new environment and watch my cat change from being lethargic to playing with his toys. I thank God for answering my prayers.

The practice of persistent prayer has led me to persistent thanksgiving, and I am now trying to be faithful in thanking God for answered prayers, big or small.

Prayer: *Faithful God, help us to be as grateful for answered prayer as we are motivated to pray for our needs. Amen*

Thought for the day: Persistence in prayer can lead to faithfulness in thanksgiving.

Cindy Smith (New York, US)

PRAYER FOCUS: THOSE LEARNING TO PRAY

Thermals of God's Love

Read Isaiah 40:28–31

Those who hope in the Lord will renew their strength. They will soar on wings like eagles; they will run and not grow weary, they will walk and not be faint.

Isaiah 40:31 (NIV)

I was on retreat in the Brecon Beacons when one day I noticed a red kite sitting in the upper branches of a tree. Then in one fluid movement he leapt from his perch and soared into the air. With wings outstretched he began to glide, effortlessly spiralling higher and higher.

A thermal was lifting him heavenwards. The wind currents rose upwards, carrying warm air into the higher, cooler reaches of the atmosphere. The kite had risen on this air escalator and within seconds was almost out of sight. All the bird needed to do was to locate the thermal and spread its wings, and the thermal did the work of lifting him.

In the same way we do not need to rely on our own strength, but on the thermals of God's love. If we align ourselves with his will and trust him, he will raise us and uphold us to become capable of more than we could ever imagine. And when we become weary, his strength will be more than sufficient to bring us rest and restore us.

Prayer: *Father, help me to rest on the thermals of your love, trusting you to lead and guide me. May it not be in my strength but yours that I seek to do your will. Amen*

Thought for the day: I can rely on God to uphold me today.

Adam Pope (Northamptonshire, England)

Rage or Blessing?

Read James 3:1–12

No human being can tame the tongue. It is a restless evil, full of deadly poison.

James 3:8 (NIV)

The words tumbled out of my mouth as I confronted my colleague. Months of pent-up frustration spilled over, becoming a raging river of anger. This man had criticised my work decisions, spoken rudely and ignored me in front of others. I thought I had forgiven him, but instead I had buried the emotions inside. As I was confronting him, my outburst offended him. Although I later asked for forgiveness, he would not speak to me.

Sometimes our tempers get the best of us. We may even use the verse quoted above to excuse our outbursts. Although we are helpless to tame our tongues, God is not. Paul cautions, 'In your anger do not sin' (Ephesians 4:26), which tells us that there are ways for us to handle anger without hurting other people.

I began to think about what I could have done differently. Months earlier, before the offences had piled up into anger, I could have calmly spoken to my colleague about our differences. Or I could have simply started asking God to bless him, which might have changed my perspective on the situation. We each have the choice of how we will respond to slights and criticism. Shall we rage, or shall we bless?

Prayer: *Dear God, help us each day to put our tongues under your control and to heed your voice. Amen*

Thought for the day: Today I will let God guide my words.

Karen Dorsey (Oregon, US)

PRAYER FOCUS: COLLEAGUES WHO STRUGGLE TO GET ON

Keep Flowing

Read Amos 5:21–24

Let justice roll on like a river, righteousness like a never-failing stream!
Amos 5:24 (NIV)

Several years ago, my wife and I spent the weekend with a friend in her new home. During our stay, she took us out into the garden to see her pond. I was struck by the stillness of the water, the water lilies and the croaking of frogs.

While reflecting on the scenic view, I had this thought: for many years I have been as still as a pond behind the grand edifice of my church. Year after year, I soaked in sermons, scripture verses and encouraging words, but I seldom let those words flow from me in service to others.

I am learning that I cannot love God fully without loving my neighbour. I love them by sharing the good news of Jesus Christ's death on the cross, praying for them, visiting them when they are sick, offering them shelter and helping them in their hour of need.

The Lord did not call us to be stagnant but to allow our faith to flow outward like a stream. Jesus said 'Whoever believes in me, as scripture has said, rivers of living water will flow from within them' (John 7:38). Water flows, the Spirit flows, love flows. Christ's love can help us transform our world as we humbly serve others inside and outside our places of worship.

Prayer: *Dear Lord, help us to be still in your presence and active in serving others. Amen*

Thought for the day: With God's help my actions can be just and righteous.

Michael Lewis (Virginia, US)

Our Strong Tower

Read Psalm 18:1–3

The name of the Lord is a fortified tower; the righteous run to it and are safe.

Proverbs 18:10 (NIV)

'Do you know how many types of chasing games there are, Mum?' my son asked. He listed various types they'd played at school. Around the dinner table, he talked with his brothers about the different types, and the difficulty of each one.

Later that evening I sat down with my youngest son, Jamie, to read the Bible. We read a portion of Psalm 18, which describes God as our fortress, our safe place. I told Jamie that God is a refuge where we can go anytime. He is like the safe place in the middle of a game of being chased. My son understood straight away. Like many children, he hides behind my legs during a chasing game and declares, 'Mum is safe!'

I prayed with him, asking that he would always run to God's safe care whenever he needs it. I prayed silently for myself too, that I would be quicker to run to God instead of trying to deal with problems on my own.

God wants us to pray about our problems and ask for his help. Even when bad things happen, we can always find refuge in his love. And we can proclaim, 'I'm safe.'

Prayer: *Dear Lord, help us remember that we can always find refuge in you. Amen*

Thought for the day: I can always find refuge in God.

Wendy Marshall (Tokyo, Japan)

Good Works

Read Titus 3:8–14
I want you to stress these things, so that those who have trusted in God may be careful to devote themselves to doing what is good.
Titus 3:8 (NIV)

Several years ago a fire destroyed a church in my town. The fire raged through the night, and firemen worked for more than 13 hours to contain it. The next day's newspaper featured an article about the fire. In the story, the church's pastor described how members of his congregation felt: 'Our members are devastated, but we know we will rebuild our church.'

Soon after the newspaper story, people from the community began donating money, furniture, musical instruments and other items to the congregation. Within two years, a brand new church had been built. Once again, the local newspaper covered the story, and it quoted church members who thanked the community for its outpouring of donations. 'I am amazed at the goodwill and love people have shared with us,' one of them said.

God's word encourages us to do good deeds and to show kindness toward others. Christ loved us so much that he gave his life for us. Through our works of love and kindness, we express our love for Christ and show that we belong to him.

Prayer: *Dear Lord, teach us how to share your gift of love with others. Give us courage to respond to the needs of your people. Amen*

Thought for the day: A chance to share God's love today is inevitable. Am I ready?

James C. Hendrix (Indiana, US)

Ash Wednesday

Read Isaiah 58:1–11

God says, 'Is not this the fast that I choose: to loose the bonds of injustice... to let the oppressed go free?'
Isaiah 58:6 (NRSV)

A year ago, when I saw that one of the meditations in The Upper Room had the title 'Ash Wednesday', I didn't really understand what that meant. I soon learned that Ash Wednesday marks the beginning of Lent, known as the 'Great Fast' in Russian Christianity. On this day some churches perform a symbolic action. The sign of the cross is made in ashes on people's foreheads as a sign of our humanity and of our need for God.

Whatever name we give this day, it is the beginning of a time of self-examination. It is not only a time to give up something we enjoy but also a time to take on some form of ministry in Christ's name. Through the prophet Isaiah God says, 'Is not this the fast that I choose: to loose the bonds of injustice, to undo the thongs of the yoke, to let the oppressed go free, and to break every yoke? Is it not to share your bread with the hungry, and bring the homeless poor into your house; when you see the naked, to cover them, and not to hide yourself from your own kin?' (Isaiah 58:6–7).

It seems, then, that the fast includes spending more time with God through prayer and reading the Bible as well as serving God through acts of love toward my neighbours. What a privilege!

Prayer: *Dear God, give us the strength and resolve to observe a genuine fast by showing justice and compassion toward our neighbours. In Jesus' name. Amen*

Thought for the day: What can I do to make Lent a true fast?

Galina Samson (Voronezh, Russia)

Walking Away From Sin

Read John 8:1–11

There is now no condemnation for those who are in Christ Jesus, because through Christ Jesus the law of the Spirit who gives life has set you free from the law of sin and death.
Romans 8:1–2 (NIV)

The woman the Pharisees dragged before Jesus was caught in adultery. The religious authorities wanted to stone her in accordance with the law. They thought they could trap Jesus by asking what he thought was the appropriate punishment. Instead of answering, he confronted their hypocrisy: 'Let any one of you who is without sin be the first to throw a stone at her.' When no one came forward, Jesus shocked them by giving the woman—and all of us—the answer needed to break free from sin: 'Then neither do I condemn you,' Jesus declared. 'Go now and leave your life of sin' (John 8:11).

I can relate to the woman in John 8:1–11. I remember the hopeless feeling of being trapped in an ongoing sin in my life. My sinful behaviour had a stranglehold on me, and I couldn't see a way out. When I realised that Jesus wanted to save me from my sin, I found the freedom I had longed for.

Jesus was not sent into this world to condemn us. Condemnation has no power to change our lives. Only when we believe and accept the forgiving grace of God and the fresh start he gives us each day can we leave our lives of sin. When we embrace the truth of God's love, our lives will never be the same.

Prayer: *Thank you, God, for not condemning but forgiving us. Thank you for setting us free to live without sin. Amen*

Thought for the day: Through loving and accepting me, God offers me a fresh start.

Chad McComas (Oregon, US)

Go for It

Read Exodus 4:1–13

Peter got down out of the boat, walked on the water and came toward Jesus. But when he saw the wind, he was afraid and, beginning to sink, cried out, 'Lord, save me!'

Matthew 14:29–30 (NIV)

My brother-in-law, Bryon, taught me how to downhill ski. As he skied backwards facing me, he told me to zig-zag across the slope so I would not gather too much speed as we descended. I was OK as long as I was traversing the slope at such a shallow angle as to creep down the ski run. But eventually I ran out of path and needed to turn back in the other direction. Changing direction meant having to point my skis straight downhill for the seconds it took to swing them around. I feared I would plummet down the slope at break-neck speed, out of control. Bryon kept urging me to turn my skis and assured me that I'd be OK. I trusted him, so finally I just said, 'Whatever happens, here goes!' and I rotated my skis around toward my opposite side. I was delighted to find myself gliding slowly in the new direction. If I hadn't trusted Bryon, I might never have learned to ski and would have missed out on much enjoyment.

To me, following God is much like that ski lesson. Sometimes we're afraid to commit to a task he has placed before us. We fear we can't do it, or we think of all the things that could go wrong. But if we truly trust God, we can take a deep breath, 'go for it', and then be amazed at what he has empowered us to do.

Prayer: *Dear Lord, help us to trust you enough to do what you call us to do and not miss out on the blessings that come from our obedience. Amen*

Thought for the day: How is God empowering me to 'go for it' today?

Debra Callaway (Kansas, US)

PRAYER FOCUS: SOMEONE LEARNING A NEW SKILL

My Strength and My Song

Read Psalm 27:1–14

Behold, God is my salvation; I will trust, and not be afraid: for the Lord Jehovah is my strength and my song; he also is become my salvation.
Isaiah 12:2 (KJV)

When my four-year-old woke up with a high temperature and fever, I didn't think I had the physical or emotional energy to deal with yet another illness. I am distressed when my children are ill because I don't want them to suffer and also because I realise that I am not in control. I can't take away their sickness or discomfort. I also need to accept that my plans must change. I will more than likely miss work to care for them, which makes stretching the next meagre pay cheque to meet our expenses more difficult.

At times like these, I can choose to focus my energy on lamenting the situation and wishing it were different, which makes me feel defeated and overwhelmed. But when I remember that 'the Lord Jehovah is my strength and my song', I feel lighter and more hopeful. I am still facing the same challenges; but when I turn to God, my spirit is lifted. I can more easily see the ways he is at work in the situation: the text message I get from a friend checking on us, a colleague who is able to cover my shift, extra moments spent with my children. Although the situation is not what I would have chosen, when I look for God's presence, I find strength and joy.

Prayer: *Dear God, when we face challenging situations, remind us that you are with us and that we can rely on you for strength. Amen*

Thought for the day: Leaning on God lightens my burdens and lifts my spirit.

Kimberly Leon (Missouri, US)

1st Sunday in Lent

Read Colossians 3:8–14

All of us are looking with unveiled faces at the glory of the Lord… [and] are being transformed into that same image.

2 Corinthians 3:18 (CEB)

Each year during Lent my church produces a musical about the life of Jesus Christ. Recently, to commemorate the 30th anniversary of the play, we invited those who had played the role of Jesus down through the years to come and stand at the altar. As each person walked up, he displayed a picture of himself in his costume. Although the actors all looked very different in person, when clothed in their costumes as Jesus, they all looked remarkably alike—making it difficult to distinguish one from the other.

In a similar way, we too can look like Christ. Not in the physical sense, but when we treat others as Christ would, help others as he did and love others as he taught, we take on Christ's image.

In our reading for today, Paul instructs the Colossians to put off worldly traits like anger, malice and filthy language. Instead, they are to put on the qualities of Christ—kindness, humility and forgiveness. Every day we can choose to look like our brother, Jesus Christ.

Prayer: *Creator of all, enable us each day to look more like Christ by renewing our hearts and minds in you. Amen*

Thought for the day: We honour God when our lives mirror Christ.

Laverne Wright (Georgia, US)

Breaking the Grip of Fear

Read Deuteronomy 31:1–8

God is our refuge and strength, a help always near in times of great trouble. That's why we won't be afraid when the world falls apart.
Psalm 46:1–2 (CEB)

While waiting for my wife to finish a doctor's appointment I took our children exploring in the massive office complex. At the bottom of one stairwell was a long corridor with cement walls, a cement floor and a windowless metal door at the end. I beckoned for the children to follow me through the damp and dimly-lit corridor toward the door, but they hesitated. The shadowy hallway and mysterious door—and what could lie on the other side—frightened them.

Then I told them that I had been through that door before. I asked them to trust me. When we opened the door, we were greeted by a burst of sunlight and the car park. 'Oh,' one of them said, 'that was nothing!'

Sometimes life can be like that dark corridor. We face uncertainty about what lies ahead and become fearful. Life may be full of trouble. But we can have confidence in our God that even if the earth shakes and trembles and the mountains fall into the sea, we are in good hands. From our perspective and limited knowledge, the situation may seem hopeless. However, God's knowledge exceeds ours. With God as our helper, our fear can give way to a sense of peace and security. Our heavenly Father knows what is on the other side of the doors in our lives, and we can trust him in all things.

Prayer: *Dear faithful God, be with those who are afraid or facing difficult circumstances. Help us to know that we can put our trust in you. Amen*

Thought for the day: Today I can take my heavenly Father's hand and go forward.

Frankie Melton (South Carolina, US)

A Chance to Live

Read John 3:13–21

God so loved the world that he gave his one and only Son, that whoever believes in him shall not perish but have eternal life. For God did not send his Son into the world to condemn the world, but to save the world through him.

John 3:16–17 (NIV)

We had been through a long dry spell that caused many people in the area to lose their crops. As I was watering my pineapple and vegetable plants, my wife asked, 'What are you doing watering withered crops that are almost certainly dying?' Without thinking, I replied that I wanted to give every seedling and plant a chance to live. Even if they dried up, I would have tried my best to ensure that they lived.

Later, I reflected on the phrase, 'chance to live', which reminded me of John 3:16. As I meditated on this passage, I thought about the deep love that God showed us in sending Jesus Christ into the world and allowing him to die for us on the cross, so that we could all have a chance of eternal life in heaven.

Unlike my pineapple and vegetable crops that could not make a choice to live, we have the ability to choose everlasting life by believing in Jesus Christ. Praise God that we all have the chance to believe and to receive salvation!

Prayer: *Dear God, thank you for giving your Son for us so that we have a chance to live eternally with you. Give us the courage to share your grace and to encourage others to make the conscious choice to believe in Jesus Christ. Amen*

Thought for the day: What can I do to help someone to know Christ and to receive the gift of eternal life?

Philip Polo (Nairobi, Kenya)

Still Changing Hearts

Read Acts 9:1–6
[God] changes times and seasons, deposes kings and sets up kings.
Daniel 2:21 (NRSV)

When our small church has a prayer meeting, the concerns vary widely—from global threats to the challenges faced by our members. One evening as we voiced our petitions, one woman named the controversial leader of a war-torn nation that was often in the headlines. 'Lord,' she prayed, 'turn his heart to you.' My immediate (and fortunately unspoken) reaction was, 'That will never happen! Let's pray for things that are possible!'

As prayer continued, I was struck by the shallowness both of my faith and of my understanding of God's power. He desires that all people repent. Does he not have the power to change any heart?

More than 2000 years ago, a man named Saul was travelling to Damascus to imprison followers of Jesus. Instead, he was confronted by the Lord—an encounter that changed the face of Christianity for ever. Once an enemy of the church, Saul, now known as Paul, became a powerful evangelist, whose letters form much of the New Testament.

I wondered as our prayer meeting continued whether some saint in Damascus centuries ago had prayed that Saul's heart would be turned toward Jesus. Imagine her joy upon learning that God had granted her request! And imagine the joy of those who thought as I did—that such a change was impossible—because they too witnessed the mercy and power of our God.

Prayer: *Almighty God, grant us a true understanding of your power to touch the lives of all people. Amen*

Thought for the day: When have I underestimated God's power?

Lisa Stackpole (Wisconsin, US)

Let There Be Light

Read Psalm 27: 1–5
The Lord is my light and my salvation.
Psalm 27:1 (NIV)

I once attended a series of Bible study groups at our church. All the members benefited from sharing insights on the Bible passages and from praying together. When I was asked to share a favourite scripture verse, I chose 'Let there be light' (Genesis 1:3).

I have been chronically ill for many years but I try to count my blessings. Being able to see, for instance, is such a precious gift. The world is a beautiful place—the sun, the flowers, trees and wildlife give us such pleasure and we can thank God for their place in his creation. I love to see the birds as they come to use the feeders outside my window, and I enjoy visits from a friend with the puppies she is training to be guide dogs for the blind.

In the hours of darkness, when often I cannot sleep, I know that in other parts of the world, people are beginning their morning devotions, a worldwide community of prayer in which I can join. The reading of scripture and the comfort of prayer can bring light into our darkest days.

Prayer: *Dear Lord, help us always to be aware of your presence in our Bible reading and in our prayer time, bringing your light to our minds and hearts. Amen*

Thought for the day: 'Your word is a lamp for my feet, a light on my path' (Psalm 119:105).

Ann Robertson (East Dunbartonshire, Scotland)

The Basic Pattern

Read Isaiah 61:10–11

My soul rejoices in my God. For he has clothed me with garments of salvation and arrayed me in a robe of his righteousness.
Isaiah 61:10 (NIV)

When I was twelve years old, all the girls in our class were required to take up sewing. We had to make three items: an apron, a short blouse with no buttons, and a skirt. For each item, everyone followed the same pattern.

As the school year ended, girls all over the school were wearing the blouses and skirts they had made, but the shared pattern was not easily recognisable. Some had made their blouses of printed fabric that coordinated with solid-colour skirts. Others had made their garments of fabrics that did not coordinate. Still others had trimmed theirs with lace or other decorations. My mother had suggested I make both garments from the same solid blue fabric so I could wear them together as a two-piece dress. The clothes looked different on everyone.

Something similar occurs in Christianity. Those of us who accept Jesus Christ as our Lord and Saviour are expected to follow basic guidelines such as the ten commandments (see Exodus 20:1–17). Although we follow the example of Jesus, Christianity looks different on each of us. We may wear it differently, but it still fits us all.

Prayer: *Dear heavenly Father, thank you for providing the pattern for salvation so that we may be clothed in righteousness and wrapped in your love. Amen*

Thought for the day: Today I will look past the differences among Christians to focus on our similarities.

Mary Hunt Webb (New Mexico, US)

Refuge

Read Psalm 90:1–17
Lord, you have been our help, generation after generation.
Psalm 90:1 (CEB)

My mother is currently in hospital because she is suffering from kidney disease. I was with her yesterday for several hours. Even though I found it difficult to understand what she was saying, when she smiled at me she radiated the love of the God she has known all her life.

My mother is a woman of prayer and reads the Bible with avid devotion every day. This year she started reading the entire Bible for the tenth time. Her faith in God has always been her refuge and her source of strength in difficult times. Her giving spirit has led her to provide shelter to the helpless, attend to the sick and feed the hungry. She has repeatedly said to us: 'My children, the legacy I leave you is to follow Christ.'

Though her medical condition is serious, I know she is secure in the arms of our Lord. Her loving example reminds us that in days of prosperity and adversity we can find refuge in God.

Prayer: *Thank you, Lord, for providing loving examples of faith. Help us to follow them, as we pray: 'Our Father which art in heaven, Hallowed be thy name. Thy kingdom come. Thy will be done in earth, as it is in heaven. Give us this day our daily bread. And forgive us our debts, as we forgive our debtors. And lead us not into temptation, but deliver us from evil: For thine is the kingdom, and the power, and the glory, for ever. Amen.'**

Thought for the day: What legacy of faith will I leave for others?

Jesus Quintanilla Osorio (Quintana Roo, Mexico)

* Matthew 6:9–13 (KJV)

2nd Sunday in Lent

Read Hebrews 4:14–16

We do not have a high priest who is unable to feel sympathy with our weaknesses, but we have one who has been tempted in every way, just as we are—yet he did not sin.

Hebrews 4:15 (NIV)

One season of Lent was especially meaningful for me because of a particular study my church offered. It helped me to relate to the thoughts and actions of many people who were present when Christ was crucified and rose from the dead. I considered the ways I deny Christ by my actions or words—the times I fall asleep when I pray, the times I fail to see God in my daily life. I identified with the doubts and fears of the disciples and I certainly identified with Christ's cry of abandonment on the cross.

Christ in his humanity experienced many trials. Because of his earthly life Christ understands and helps me when I experience pain, suffering, doubt or feelings of abandonment. Christ is with me to help me endure my own trials. How grateful I am that we serve a risen Saviour who has walked where we walk and who continues to walk with us today!

Prayer: *Heavenly Father, thank you for the gift of your Son. Thank you for understanding our weaknesses and help us to work through them as you live in us and walk with us. Amen*

Thought for the day: Christ understands and will help me with my weaknesses.

Brenda Alford (Florida, US)

Living Water

Read John 4:4–15

Jesus answered her, 'If you knew the gift of God and who it is that asks you for a drink, you would have asked him and he would have given you living water.'

John 4:10 (NIV)

Water is essential to life. It makes up 50–75 per cent of our bodies, yet we often forget to drink enough water or we substitute it with other drinks which do us little good. As a result, many of us spend our days slightly dehydrated.

I love the parallel between these facts and what Jesus says in scripture: 'Everyone who drinks this water will be thirsty again, but whoever drinks the water I give them will never thirst. Indeed, the water I give them will become in them a spring of water welling up to eternal life' (John 4:13–14).

Recently, I created a new daily practice to make these thoughts tangible. When I get out of bed and make my way to the bathroom, I pick up a special glass I've placed next to the basin. While I fill up the glass, I turn my mind to Christ. In gratitude, I sip slowly, thanking him for the life he offers me through this water and his living water. This practice reminds me that Jesus is the source of my life and that I need to spend time with God—the 'living water' that sustains me.

Prayer: *Dear God, help us to remember that our lives are better when we drink deeply of your living water. Amen*

Thought for the day: Today when I drink water, I will remember the power of Christ's living water.

Caryl Moll (Randburg, South Africa)

PRAYER FOCUS: THOSE WHO LACK ACCESS TO CLEAN WATER

Worship While You Work

Read Colossians 3:15–17

Since, then, you have been raised with Christ, set your hearts on things above, where Christ is, seated at the right hand of God. Set your minds on things above, not on earthly things.
Colossians 3:1–2 (NIV)

Carrying a bucket of cleaning things, I trudged to clean the campsite bathrooms for what seemed like the fiftieth time. The sun had set on a long day of work; and to combat a drooping spirit, I began singing favourite praise songs. In one song, the lyrics asked for a worshipful attitude that honours God from morning to evening. While repeating the words, I smiled a little, thinking about exalting the king of kings while cleaning mirrors and scrubbing toilets.

The song list continued with Philippians 4:13 set to music, which motivated me to finish with a smile and diligent hands. Despite feeling weary, I shifted my focus to set my mind on things above. While sweeping the floor, I remembered a well-known truth: believers can worship God anywhere. While singing to the creator and wiping down the sinks, I realised that Christians don't need to be in a church with music to glorify God, but can proclaim his awesome name in the middle of any mundane job.

Prayer: *Dear Lord, thank you for leading us to glorify you no matter where we are. Amen*

Thought for the day: No matter where we are, we can worship God.

Lauren Williams (Indiana, US)

Father's Delight

Read Zephaniah 3:14–17

The Lord takes delight in his people; he crowns the humble with victory.
Psalm 149:4 (NIV)

As a new grandma, I love watching my son with his daughter. His eyes sparkle and he grins from ear to ear, rejoicing in her existence. Even if she is sick on his shirt, he hugs her, laughs and says, 'You overflowed!'

My own dad did not always delight in me. Sometimes I snuggled on his lap. But at other times I was afraid of him. Human fathers aren't perfect. They may love and enjoy their children, or they may neglect, abuse and abandon them. Calling God 'Father' can be difficult for me. Since I had to work so hard to please my dad, I feel that I need to work hard to please God.

My son has become my example. Watching him with his baby shows me the Bible's picture of our heavenly Father. Zephaniah 3:17 (CEB) says, 'The Lord your God is in your midst… He will create calm with his love; he will rejoice over you with singing.' Imagine God singing to us! Psalm 18:19 (NIV) says, 'He rescued me because he delighted in me.' We can turn to our heavenly Father without fear. We don't need to work to please God. We can talk about anything and everything. He loves us and takes delight in us. Thinking about his love makes me smile all day.

Prayer: *Dear God, thank you for rejoicing over us with singing. Let our lives reflect your joy. Amen*

Thought for the day: How will I respond to God's delight in me?

Jane Reid (Oregon, US)

Seeds are for Sowing

Read Galatians 5:22–26

Examine yourselves to see whether you are living in the faith. Test yourselves.

2 Corinthians 13:5 (NRSV)

On the island where my husband and I live the weather becomes very hot during the summer. To alleviate the effects of the morning heat, I prepare refreshing passion-fruit drinks for us. The fruit comes from the vines in our garden. One day as I gathered the fruit, I noticed a vine that had only a single fruit. But it was absolutely beautiful—glossy, big and healthy-looking. I thought it would be wonderful and more than sufficient for two people. What a disappointment to find that when I cut it open, the fruit was hollow! It had a beautiful outer appearance but no flesh for eating or seeds for sowing.

After a bit of introspection, I thought of the need for Christians to be genuine and active, not to worry about appearances. We have been called to serve others, to act upon the fruit of the Spirit given to us according to Galatians 5. Let us gather sufficient seeds of the gospel to plant where they are needed as Christ has called us to do.

Prayer: *Creator God, may we live and be guided by the Spirit to sow the seeds of the gospel. Help us examine ourselves so that we can be constantly reminded of the life you would have us live. In Christ's name we pray. Amen*

Thought for the day: When I sow the seeds of the gospel with love, God gathers the harvest.

Maria M. Urdaz (Carolina, Puerto Rico)

How Do We Respond?

Read John 6:1–14

Jesus said to Philip, 'Where are we to buy bread for these people to eat?'
John 6:5 (NRSV)

In today's passage, Jesus asks Philip where the disciples could buy bread to feed the multitude that had been following Jesus. The scripture says that Jesus asks Philip the question in order to 'test him'—to see how he would respond.

Jesus already knew what he was going to do about feeding the crowd. But he wanted to see if Philip would respond with faith or with doubt. Philip did not take into account what Jesus could do to solve the problem. Philip saw what was possible through human efforts, not what was possible through the involvement of Jesus.

What about us? Do we look at our life's struggles with a limited viewpoint as Philip did? Or do we view them based on what is possible when our heavenly Father gets involved?

The next time we are faced with a problem or crisis, will we rely on our limited strength, knowledge and capabilities? Or will we prayerfully involve our heavenly Father in the situation? When we offer our struggles to God, we can see that his incredible power brings us solutions we never thought possible.

Prayer: *Almighty God, help us always to look to you when problems arise, trusting you to do what we cannot. Amen*

Thought for the day: No problem is too big for God.

Terry Sexton (Tennessee, US)

Walking on Eggshells

Read Psalm 32:1–11

The one the Lord doesn't consider guilty—in whose spirit there is no dishonesty—that one is truly happy!
Psalm 32:2 (CEB)

While I am caring for my grandparents I sometimes feel as if I am walking on eggshells. Their burdens are so heavy with physical pain, emotional anxiety and mental confusion that I don't share my own burdens with them for fear of troubling them. Hearing anything negative easily upsets them, which makes being completely authentic difficult in their company.

I never need to walk on eggshells with God. After a trying day of fetching medicines, scrubbing floors and washing laundry, I'm welcome to fling my whole self into God's arms: frustrations, worries, doubts, sin, questions, as well as praises and thanksgiving. I can't surprise, hide from or deceive God. All my troubles are small compared to the Lord's infinite wisdom and power.

Christ died and rose again that we might enjoy full access to God through the Holy Spirit and be known and loved completely. Nothing can taint or diminish divine love. When we throw our hearts into God's embrace through prayer, he showers us with abundant love.

Prayer: *Dear God, thank you for embracing us exactly as we are. Amen*

Thought for the day: I need hold nothing back from God.

Megan Anderson (Indiana, US)

3rd Sunday in Lent

Read Philippians 3:20–21

Be transformed by the renewing of your minds, so that you may discern what is the will of God.

Romans 12:2 (NRSV)

'I'm afraid I don't like change!' It was a comment a member of our congregation had often expressed in church meetings when we discussed different styles of worship or new approaches to our gospel mission. This time a loving friend replied, 'I'm sorry about that. What are you going to do when you die?' We remembered Paul's words, 'We will not all die, but we will all be changed' (1 Corinthians 15:51).

Resistance to change has often been a divisive stumbling block for both church and society. Change may not always be good, but our life in Christ is a journey through change. Through God's renewing grace we reflect our new life in Christ in our thoughts and attitudes. As we mature in faith, life becomes a day-by-day transformation into the likeness of Christ.

A few months after I went through a personal deepening experience of Jesus as Saviour and Lord, a close family member said to me, 'You're different!' I want that sort of change to continue. When we embrace change we allow the Holy Spirit to work in us, helping us to mature spiritually.

Prayer: *Dear God, keep changing us. Renew our hearts and minds constantly. Help us to have openness and wisdom in the face of every change. Amen*

Thought for the day: Today I will welcome changes that come from drawing close to Jesus.

Colin Harbach (Carlisle, England)

God Working in Me

Read Philippians 2:12–18

It is God who works in you to will and to act in order to fulfil his good purpose.
Philippians 2:13 (NIV)

We have all experienced a time when something in life concerns us. A problem may arise and we wonder why someone can't solve it. Or a charitable cause may speak to us, and we ask why people don't give more of their time and money.

Not long ago, my church started to lose many of its young members. Some stopped attending, while others married and moved away. And our church wasn't attracting new young members. What was wrong with us? Was it the music? Did our activities fail to target the 20-something age group? I couldn't work it out. I talked to my family, demanding to know why the congregation wasn't doing more to welcome younger people to our church.

Philippians 2:13 helped me realise that God doesn't call everyone for every purpose. He works in each of us in different ways. In meditating on these words, I realised that while I was waiting for others to do something, God was urging me to help my church to attract younger people. He was working in me for this specific purpose. I simply needed to answer his call.

Prayer: *Dear God, help us recognise and respond to your call so that we may work according to your purpose. Amen*

Thought for the day: What is God calling me to do?

Jennifer Brigandi (Ontario, Canada)

By the time you read this I will have been in the position of acquisitions editor of *The Upper Room* magazine for almost a year. I live on the family farm in Charlotte, Tennessee, a small town west of Nashville. I grew up in the hayfields and shallow creeks among the cows, poplars and limestone common to this part of the country. Physically, spiritually and intellectually, I was formed here—surrounded by family, hard work and a strong community of godly men and women bent on living lives of exemplary faith and passing on that faith from generation to generation.

Growing up, I spent summers in the hayfields with my grandfather. My front window looks out over one of those fields, and one evening not long ago I found myself pondering all that has occurred between those summers of my youth and the present. What did I imagine—back then—that my life would be? What is the reality of my life now?

Back then, I would not have imagined myself involved in ministry in any formal setting, which for me largely meant being a preacher at a church. Later in my life I realised that ministry is not confined to the pulpit. God calls some people to preach at a church. Others are called to volunteer at a prison or a homeless shelter. My ministry is helping writers give expression to their ideas and experiences in a way that contributes to the personal and collective prayers of *The Upper Room* readers throughout the world.

As Christians, we are a people of prayer—in all its depth, dimension and variety. Our prayers take many different forms. For much of my childhood and youth, praying involved either reciting the short, rhyming verses memorised and spoken aloud before a meal or bedtime or the longer, more elegant prayers I heard uttered in my country church. However, I have learned over time that prayer also includes our sighs and groans, our moments of frustration and weakness, and even those periods of silence when we rack our brains for the right words but cannot seem to find them.

At some moments in my life I have struggled to pray. I have not always been confident that my prayers are heard or that what I am praying for is in fact what I need to be praying for. At other times I have gone through long, dry stretches during which I have said very little to God. But I like to think that in my better moments, I have prayed continually and with confidence, although not without the help and encouragement of people like you. This is why we find ourselves in the pages of this magazine: to pray together, to offer encouragement, to help one another find the words when they escape us.

As both a reader of *The Upper Room* and part of the staff of the English edition, I belong to a family that extends across the globe, a family of readers and writers all working toward the same end—to share concerns, struggles and disappointments; faith, joy and witness; moments of clarity, confusion or some combination of both. Ours is a community of people defined neither by location nor language, race nor nationality, but by our common concern for one another, joined together in prayer. And while back in the hayfield I would not have imagined myself here, where I have ended up is better than where I thought I was going. It is good to be among you.

Questions for Reflection:

1. What does the word 'ministry' mean to me? What actions do I engage in that would be considered ministry?

2. Have there been moments in my life when I have struggled to pray? Who or what encouraged me to keep going?

3. What does it mean to me to be part of a community joined together in prayer?

Andrew Garland Breeden
Acquisitions Editor

From Fear to Strength

Read Psalm 91:14–16

Do not fear, for I am with you; do not be dismayed, for I am your God. I will strengthen you and help you; I will uphold you with my righteous right hand.

Isaiah 41:10 (NIV)

When my late husband developed a debilitating disease in his mid-thirties that would gradually paralyse him over a 24-year period, I was afraid of what the future might hold. How would we make our living? How would the disease affect our children and our marriage? As the disease progressed and my husband's abilities diminished, we had to search continually for ways to adjust to his new limitations.

One of the blessings of this adversity was that through these difficult times, we sought a closer relationship with God. As I look back, I can see that even when we prayed for physical healing, which didn't come, God was with us—strengthening and blessing our marriage and our family relationships, sustaining us through financial hardships and upholding us through many trials. Life is not always easy, but we can trust in God's promise to strengthen us and to help us.

Prayer: *Thank you, God, for loving us. Help us to put our trust in you, knowing that you will strengthen us and help us through difficult times. Amen*

Thought for the day: When I am afraid, God invites me to pray.

Amy Arlene Anderson (Minnesota, US)

Try a Little Kindness

Read 2 Peter 1:1–8

What does the Lord require of you but to do justice, and to love kindness, and to walk humbly with your God?

Micah 6:8 (NRSV)

Many years ago I served as a deckhand on a tugboat in the waters of Tampa Bay. One of the deckhand's duties is to throw a coiled, heavy line on to a metal or wooden post of a barge and secure it. A deckhand's failure to execute this procedure correctly is very frustrating for the captain. He may have to circle and make another approach. At first I often messed up this job, until I received the following tip from an experienced hand: 'Don't try to lasso the post; just throw the coiled line at it and the loop will fall into place on its own.' This proved to be good advice and I never again had trouble with this task.

My memory of this experience reminds me of the times I've made clumsy attempts to 'lasso' non-Christians by trying to convert them. Today's verse tells us that this approach is not what the Lord requires of us. And Jesus' approach seems to have been focused on attraction rather than promotion. He healed the sick and he genuinely loved and cared about people.

I believe it is fine to invite people to church or to share the gospel. But in most cases the best way to bring others to Christ may be to try a little kindness and allow the Holy Spirit to lead us forward from there.

Prayer: *O Lord, guide us as we share your love to make disciples of all people. Amen*

Thought for the day: How can I follow the Holy Spirit in my actions today?

Scott Wierenga (Michigan, US)

Why Worry?

Read Luke 12:22–31
Do not worry about anything, but in everything by prayer and supplication with thanksgiving let your requests be made known to God.
Philippians 4:6 (NRSV)

Spring had arrived in South Africa. Looking out my window after my daily devotional that morning, I was blessed to see a beautiful display of flowers in full bloom. Trees were also beautifully adorned in a glorious spring gift of greenery.

As I enjoyed this moment, I remembered the words of Jesus: 'Why do you worry about clothes? Notice how the lilies in the field grow. They don't wear themselves out with work, and they don't spin cloth. But I say to you that even Solomon in all of his splendour wasn't dressed like one of these' (Matthew 6:28–29, CEB).

Certainly we should be responsible and concerned about issues that affect us. But when we are consumed by worry, we can commit these concerns in faith and prayer to the Lord and then listen for God's answer in our Bible readings, in our daily devotions and in meeting in worship and fellowship with Christian friends. When we are worried, we can remember these practices and trust in God's promises.

Prayer: *Loving God, thank you for your faithfulness, day by day and season by season. Help us to trust you always in all circumstances and to be faithful in prayer each day. Amen*

Thought for the day: Today I will bring my worries to God in prayer.

Alec Stoltz (Gauteng, South Africa)

Making Excuses

Read John 5:1–9

Jesus… asked [the sick man], 'Do you want to get well?' 'Sir,' the invalid replied, 'I have no one to help me into the pool when the water is stirred. While I am trying to get in, someone else goes down ahead of me.'
John 5:6–7 (NIV)

The man in today's reading had been sick for 38 years. He had suffered all that time, hoping for a cure—or just wanting a friend to lift him into the healing waters that he thought could make him well. Then Jesus came by and asked him a simple question: 'Do you want to get well?' The man didn't yell, 'Yes, of course I want to get well!' at the top of his voice as we might expect. Instead, he gave an explanation for why he hadn't been made well up to this point.

We also may try to explain or even make excuses: why we were late for work, didn't finish a project on time or can't change something in our lives. We can come up with a million excuses for why we can't follow God. For me, those excuses include: I don't have enough time, I'm too busy, I don't have enough money or I'm too afraid. Sometimes it seems we can't even imagine the ways in which God can change us.

In today's reading, Jesus listened to the man's explanation and then healed him, then and there. When we come to Jesus and ask to change, to be made well, we can lay down our excuses. And then we can begin to walk side by side with Jesus in a life more abundant than we could ever imagine.

Prayer: *Dear God, thank you for listening to us and calling us to change in ways we cannot now imagine. Amen*

Thought for the day: God is patiently drawing me closer.

Stephanie Marker (Missouri, US)

In His Footsteps

Read 1 Peter 2:19–25
Christ suffered for you, leaving you an example, that you should follow in his steps.
1 Peter 2:21 (NIV)

When I was six, I experienced my first blizzard. Imagine my shock when Dad opened the door revealing over a foot of snow! We seemed to be trapped. 'How can we ever get out?' I exclaimed.

'Don't worry,' Dad answered. 'I'll clear the way.' With that, he kicked the snow from the doorstep and began to shovel the snow from the path. I kept behind him each step of the way, and I was soon outdoors enjoying the sunshine and playing in the snow. Getting outside hadn't been hard at all. Dad did all the work; I needed only to follow in his footsteps.

Someone else has also gone before us to clear the way, our Lord Jesus Christ. From time to time, 'blizzards' of all types come into our lives. They can cause us to feel just as trapped as I did by that blizzard. Yet, when we turn to Christ and allow him to lead the way, we can emerge from our trials into the sunlight of a better day.

Prayer: *Dear Lord, when faced with a frightening situation, may we put our fears aside, turn to you in faith and allow you to lead the way toward better circumstances. Amen*

Thought for the day: Today and every day I will trust Jesus Christ to guide my steps.

Monica A. Andermann (New York, US)

4th Sunday in Lent

Read Acts 3:24–26

The Lord is longsuffering, and of great mercy, forgiving iniquity and transgression, and by no means clearing the guilty, visiting the iniquity of the fathers upon the children unto the third and fourth generation.
Numbers 14:18 (KJV)

I bought a horse that was about twelve years old with a bad knee. He was too old to race, not good with cattle and not good to ride. Yet I paid a good price for him. I bought him for his lineage, the bloodlines of his ancestors that he would pass down to the colts he fathered. Because of his bloodlines, he could be expected to pass down the traits of a good horse that would win races. In the horse industry, the best indication of a new colt's quality is what he inherits from his ancestors.

In the same way, parents pass down many physical characteristics to their biological children. But the examples we set for those around us often have an even greater influence on their lives. Prejudice or indifference toward others might be passed down in a community for many generations. Because children learn much from observation, we can all influence the lives of children, even if we have none of our own. And so it is with God's children.

Jesus Christ came to save the world and to set an example of sacrificial love for us to follow. As Christians, we should strive to set a similar example for those around us. When younger generations receive Christ-like spiritual and moral messages from the adults who influence their lives, they can receive good traits, a strong foundation and a legacy that will continue for many generations.

Prayer: *Dear Lord, help us to set a Christ-like example for others. Amen*

Thought for the day: Christ-like words and actions help children to live faithfully.

B.J. Woods (Texas, US)

Come!

Read Matthew 11:28–30
Jesus said, 'Come to me, all you who are weary and burdened, and I will give you rest.'
Matthew 11:28 (NIV)

'Jonathan, come downstairs for lunch,' I called to my four-year-old grandson.

'OK, Grandma,' Jonathan answered, but he didn't come.

I called again and again. Each time I received the same verbal response but no action. Finally, I went up, took his hand, and walked him down the stairs. 'When Grandma calls you, it's not enough to hear. You must come,' I told him.

Then I realised that I needed to take my own advice as I struggled with concerns about my mother. I was in the process of moving her from her home to a retirement home, and felt overwhelmed with worries. Will she adjust? What will happen if she doesn't?

In this experience with my grandson I saw God's message to me: it was not enough for me to know from scripture that he offers me rest from my worries. I need to respond to the invitation to bring my worries to him in prayer. In the case of my mother, that meant praying about my anxiety over her move and trusting God to give me wisdom.

It is the same with any worry we have. We can pray about each concern and ask God to show us the way through. Then, we can let go of the problem and rest, knowing that he will lead us to a solution.

Prayer: *Dear Lord, we come to you now with our worries. Help us give them to you and trust that you will guide us through them. Amen*

Thought for the day: God is calling me. How will I respond?

Geneva Cobb Iijima (Oregon, US)

The Mist and the Mountain

Read Psalm 121:1–8

Why, my soul, are you downcast? Why so disturbed within me? Put your hope in God, for I will yet praise him, my Saviour and my God.
Psalm 43:5 (NIV)

We used to live near a mountain, and I enjoyed glancing at it in admiration whenever I drove to a nearby town. One morning, the day was wet and misty as I set off; when I looked for the mountain, it had completely disappeared. I had no beautiful view to enjoy as I drove along. Later, the sun came out and cleared away the rain and mist; so by the time I returned home, the mountain was clearly visible again. It had been there all the time, of course. I couldn't see it because it was completely obscured by rain clouds. Only when they were cleared away could I see the mountain again.

I remembered how distant God seems when we are going through difficult times, as if we are alone. But we aren't. God is with us, and we can call to the Lord even if we don't feel his presence. God is faithful. He never leaves us.

Prayer: *Dear Lord, thank you for always being at hand to help us, even when we are not aware of your presence. As Jesus taught us, we pray, 'Our Father in heaven, hallowed be your name, your kingdom come, your will be done, on earth as it is in heaven. Give us today our daily bread. And forgive us our debts, as we also have forgiven our debtors. And lead us not into temptation, but deliver us from the evil one. Amen.'**

Thought for the day: Faith continues to hope, even when God seems distant.

Elaine Brown (Perthshire, Scotland)

* Matthew 6:9–13 (NIV)

A Bond of Support

Read 2 Corinthians 1:8–11

On [God] we have set our hope that he will continue to deliver us, as you help us by your prayers.
2 Corinthians 1:10–11 (NIV)

The winter of 2014 was rough. In addition to the snow and ice, my wife, Kathryn, spent three weeks in the hospital and came home showing no improvement. Then two weeks later, she died.

During the bleakest days of my wife's illness, I did what was necessary to help her. Often I thought of Paul's words to his Corinthian friends when he reminded them of the hardships he suffered. In that situation, he was 'under great pressure, far beyond [his] ability to endure, so that [he] despaired of life itself' (2 Corinthians 1:8, NIV). In the situation I faced, I was surely under pressure, but I was not where Paul was.

In those weeks, when I had opportunity to do so, I went to my computer and read the messages that came from around the world reassuring me that people were praying for us. Then I remembered the other words of Paul, 'You help us by your prayers', and I was strengthened.

When we become united by the prayers of our friends, we establish a strong and powerful supporting bond that brings us encouragement and enables us to bear even the heaviest burdens.

Prayer: *Thank you, loving Father, for the supporting bond of prayer that comes from caring friends. In the name of Christ, our Lord, we pray. Amen*

Thought for the day: The prayers of friends can be a powerful healing force.

Howard Coop (Kentucky, US)

Hidden Treasures

Read Matthew 25:14–29

The man who had received one bag went off, dug a hole in the ground and hid his master's money.

Matthew 25:18 (NIV)

Years ago, I boxed up my collection of antique dolls and stored them in the loft. Some time later a friend invited my daughter to attend a week-long medical mission trip to Jamaica. As we wondered how we might raise the needed funds, it occurred to me that I could sell my doll collection on the internet. As I took the dolls out of their dusty boxes, I recalled how I once enjoyed displaying them. I also thought of the servant who hid his master's money in Jesus' parable of the talents. I began to feel as if I had been doing the same thing by 'hiding' these treasures in my loft when they could be invested in a good cause.

I sold the antique dolls and shortly had enough to pay for the mission trip, where my daughter worked with orphans, aided a dentist and visited patients in a hospital. She returned beaming and transformed.

My hobby of selling on the internet has blossomed into a mission project for our church—selling donated collectables that have been in cupboards, cellars and lofts. I have also helped to establish a scholarship fund for college students serving on humanitarian mission trips. Our efforts have raised a great deal of money in five years. Digging up my 'buried talent' has reaped more rewards than I ever could have imagined.

Prayer: *Generous provider, thank you for gifts of love, compassion and the desire to serve. May we share these gifts with others. Amen*

Thought for the day: Where can I discover hidden gifts from God?

Cynthia Zimbelman-Burr (Kansas, US)

A Great Gift

Read Genesis 2:7–15

The earth is the Lord's, and everything in it, the world, and all who live in it.
Psalm 24:1 (NIV)

Out for a walk the other day, I came across an area full of stately trees. As I continued on my walk I suddenly noticed rubbish strewn about that ruined the look of the area. Instead of looking at the wonderful beauty of creation, all one could see was old bits of paper, cans and food wrappers.

Quite often I say that to be a Christian means to pray, repent and have a close relationship with God. Certainly this is true, but sometimes we fail to talk about caring for God's creation. It is a temporary gift, a loan, of such importance that we must daily remember it—and remember the One who offered it to us in the first place.

God created this beautiful earth with such dedication and love and then entrusted it to us. Rather than squander this gift, we can resolve to care for, nurture and cherish it.

Prayer: *Creator God, help us to dedicate ourselves to the task of caring for and preserving your creation. We pray in the name of Jesus. Amen*

Thought for the day: How can I be a better steward of God's magnificent creation?

Cristy Gabriele Taveras Rodríguez (Dominican Republic)

Peer Pressure

Read 2 Corinthians 5:11–21

If anyone is in Christ, there is a new creation: everything old has passed away; see, everything has become new!
2 Corinthians 5:17 (NRSV)

'Do you want to try some of this?' someone at the party asked me.

'No, I don't do drugs.' Though I was tempted to go along with the crowd, I knew that involvement with drugs could lead to health problems, perhaps even drug addiction. It could lead to legal problems and a police record. I want to avoid damaging my health and my standing in the community. Even more, I want to set an example that reflects my faith and will help others to avoid such problems.

I have many shortcomings, and I'm far from perfect. But I believe that I am called to help other people, and that includes letting people know that I am against this kind of behaviour. According to 2 Corinthians 5:17, in Christ I am a new creation. I want my lifestyle to reflect the image of Christ. When I do the wrong thing, I must repent, ask for forgiveness and change my behaviour. With God's help, I can progress and grow stronger in my Christian faith.

My relationship with Christ must go beyond church attendance to include sincere prayer, listening to God's guidance and setting an example to others.

Prayer: *Dear Lord, thank you for helping us to stay open to your leading and guidance. In Jesus' name, we pray. Amen*

Thought for the day: How will I set a Christian example today?

William J. Thomas (Kansas, US)

5th Sunday in Lent

Read Jeremiah 29:10–14

'I know the plans I have for you,' declares the Lord, 'plans to prosper you and not to harm you, plans to give you hope and a future.'
Jeremiah 29:11 (NIV)

Running puts me directly in the midst of God's beautiful Great Smoky Mountains. One of my favourite trails leads me to a cliff top where I can see for many miles. One misty morning after rain, I found myself looking out into the distance only to find that the mist had obscured several mountain ranges. I could see the range closest to me but not the other ridges that I knew were beyond it.

In the same way that I wanted to see beyond the range closest to me, most of us would like to see beyond the present. I am thinking about retiring and wonder if I invested enough to do so. Will health issues become a problem? Can I remain independent or will I have to rely on others? Regardless of age, any of us can worry about the future. I learned from my experience of the 'missing' mountain ridges that even when I cannot see them, I can know that God has plans for my future. And though the future will bring challenges, we can be assured that he will be there to see us through them.

Prayer: *Dear Father, we thank you for the future, whatever may come. We are blessed to know that you will be with us through both happy and difficult times. We pray in the name of your Son, Jesus. Amen*

Thought for the day: During each stage of my journey, God will be with me.

Julia Jones Price (Tennessee, US)

God's Blessings

Read Zephaniah 3:9–20
For the Lord God is a sun and shield; the Lord bestows favour and honour; no good thing does he withhold from those whose way of life is blameless.
Psalm 84:11 (NIV)

Over the years, my perspective on God's blessings has changed. I used to believe that disobedience would result in God's bringing us to repentance by withholding blessings. While I still believe that God may sometimes withhold blessings, I have come to realise that our attitudes and actions may prevent us, rather, from fully accepting his blessings.

The love of family and friends is one of God's greatest blessings; after all, God is love. However, I have found that I appreciate that blessing most often when I am patient, loving and kind; I appreciate it least when I have a bad attitude, use harsh words, act inconsiderately or fail to treat people with respect.

The flow of God's blessings in my life is rather like the flow of water through a pipe. My attitude and actions affect whether I experience God's blessings flowing freely or as a trickle. Now I regularly ask myself if my attitudes and actions are keeping clear or blocking up the pipes for God's blessing.

Prayer: *Dear God, help us to remain open to your blessings so that we can share them freely with others. Amen*

Thought for the day: Am I open to receive God's blessings?

William George Gosling (Western Australia, Australia)

The Race to be Last

Read Philippians 2:1–11

The greatest among you will be your servant. For those who exalt themselves will be humbled, and those who humble themselves will be exalted.

Matthew 23:11–12 (NIV)

'First one to the car wins!' My competitive children, aged four and six, raced out the door, down the steps and across the drive to the door of the car. The victorious shout of 'I win!' from one child was followed by a cry of despair from the other. When I opened the door, the competition continued with them trying to determine who could buckle their seatbelt faster.

One day, my husband told them that Jesus said, 'The last will be first, and the first will be last' (Matthew 20:16). From then on, they tried to be the last to the car and the last to buckle their seatbelt. When they each refused to buckle their seatbelts until the other one did, I was sure we weren't going to leave the drive at all that day. I was frustrated by their standoff but encouraged that they'd applied the lesson, even if they were taking it a little too literally.

To be honest, I don't want to be last. I don't want to be left out of anything. But Jesus is clear that those who humble themselves are honoured in the end. In today's reading, Paul instructed the early Christians to think of others first. If I want my life to look more like Jesus' life, then I have to rid myself of the desire to be first. Like my children, I can strive to be last, not because I think nothing of myself but because I think more of others.

Prayer: *Dear God, when we want to be first, show us how we can humbly serve others. In Jesus' name, we pray. Amen*

Thought for the day: We become more like Christ when we put others first.

Lisa Bartelt (Pennsylvania, US)

Customised Devotions

Read Psalm 119:10–16

The word is very near to you; it is in your mouth and in your heart for you to observe.
Deuteronomy 30:14 (NRSV)

When I first turned to *The Upper Room* as a spiritual resource, I was too lazy to look up the scripture readings that begin each day's meditation (a mistake I've since corrected), and I spent little, if any, time praying for those featured in each 'prayer focus'. But gradually, faith-filled anecdotes and insights shared by believers around the world have touched and transformed my spirit. I have come to love pondering the daily message and praying the prayers.

Recently, I added a new twist to my devotional time. I read the day's scripture passage, sit back, close my eyes and 'write' my own meditation. I think of a situation in my life where the scripture has applied or might be applied. I try to distil my meditation into a 'thought for the day' or an action step I can take. And I pray for an appropriate group of people or some part of my own life that especially needs God's power. Then I go on to finish reading that day's entry in the magazine. Now I get a double blessing every time I use *The Upper Room*.

Prayer: *Dear God, thank you for the opportunity to engage with scripture in new ways each day. In Jesus' name. Amen*

Thought for the day: God's word is a lamp for our feet, a light for our path (see Psalm 119:105).

Carla Haddix (Florida, US)

Rejoicing over Us

Read Jeremiah 9:23–24

They will say to Jerusalem, 'The Lord your God… will take great delight in you, he will quiet you with his love, he will rejoice over you with singing.'
Zephaniah 3:16–17 (NIV)

I remember the first time I held my newborn daughter. I rejoiced over her by singing and offering prayers and praises of thanksgiving as tears of joy streamed from my eyes. Cuddling the tiny bundle, I took her on her first dance around the hospital room.

Through the years, as she grew, we continued to dance. When she was a young child I would pick her up, hold her tightly and sing songs to her. I was excited that she was alive. Recently she asked if I would let her stand on my feet as we danced. Holding her close, I slowly danced her around the room. I enjoyed rejoicing over her once again.

The Bible tells us that just as parents delight in their children, God rejoices over us. The Bible promises that God's nearness and love are constant. We can sense our Creator's presence through any blessing that a day may bring, whether it is the companionship of a pet, the beauty of a sunrise or a surprise visit from a friend. Even on days when nothing helps us to sense God's love, we act on what we know to be true—that he is constant and trustworthy—and then trust that the knowledge of his love will follow. On days when we feel neglected or alone, the Lord's promises bring us hope and challenge us to keep going.

Prayer: *Loving Father, make us aware of your presence today. Thank you for rejoicing over us and loving us. Amen*

Thought for the day: God is nearby and takes delight in me.

Rhett Wilson (South Carolina, US)

Spiritual Exercise

Read James 2:14–26

Strengthen your drooping hands and weak knees! Make straight paths for your feet so that if any part is lame, it will be healed rather than injured more seriously.
Hebrews 12:12–13 (CEB)

At the age of 51, I decided to buy a bicycle. I had always loved cycling but had not been on a bike for more than 20 years. My only reservation was that I had experienced a few knee problems, and I was concerned that bike riding might make things worse. After a month of regular cycling, however, my knees were better than they had been in years. The exercise had strengthened the muscles so that my knees were better supported and I was less prone to injury.

Just as physical exercise helps strengthen our bodies, spiritual exercise can strengthen our spiritual muscles. Bible study, prayer and Christian fellowship are a great start, but we also need to exercise our faith in other ways. This may mean applying a biblical truth to a specific situation, such as giving food to a needy neighbour. It could mean being obedient when God calls us to a certain task or ministry, even though we feel ill-equipped for that role. When we exercise our faith, our spirits will be strengthened as we see God work in us and through us. When we trust him to give us strength, we'll be amazed at the results.

Prayer: *Dear Lord, please help us to give as much attention to our spiritual health as our physical health so that we can serve you with all that we are. Amen*

Thought for the day: What can I do today to exercise my spiritual muscles?

Nola Passmore (Queensland, Australia)

PRAYER FOCUS: CYCLISTS

Please and Thank You

Read Psalm 107:1–9

O give thanks to the Lord, for he is good; for his steadfast love endures for ever.

Psalm 107:1 (NRSV)

When I was a child, my mother and father taught me the importance of the words 'please' and 'thank you'. Over the past 60 plus years, I've learned again and again just how powerful these words can be both in conversation and in prayer.

Reflecting recently on my daily prayers, I found myself using the word 'please' frequently—very frequently in fact. I used the words 'thank you', too, but not as often. I realised that my petitions and requests were far more numerous than my expressions of gratefulness and appreciation for the blessings God has already provided. Wanting to change that, I decided to begin silently saying 'Thank you!' throughout the day—every time I sense God's presence or every time I experience one of his blessings.

As a result of a more purposeful focus on my expressions of gratitude, the power of those simple words my parents taught me decades ago has been renewed. My silent acknowledgements of God's boundless blessings throughout the day are a vivid and pleasant reminder of his care and constant presence. As we say please and thank you to God, we are continually reminded of his amazing grace, peace and steadfast love that endure for ever!

Prayer: *O God, help us cultivate a spirit of thankfulness that we may forever remain grateful for your gifts—even life itself. Amen*

Thought for the day: Gratitude is an important part of prayer.

Michael R. McGough (Pennsylvania, US)

Palm Sunday

Read Luke 19:28–40

As [the two disciples] were untying the colt, its owners asked them, 'Why are you untying the colt?' They replied, 'The Lord needs it.'
Luke 19:33–34 (NIV)

The idea of a stranger approaching me to ask for my colt (or car, or bike) was odd, if not downright comical. I never expected to experience something like the owner of the colt in Luke 19 did until one cold February night when a woman approached me as I was filling my car with petrol at a garage. She was kind as she introduced herself, but I thought that I knew where the conversation was going. My suspicions were confirmed when the woman asked me for money; I turned her down and went about my business.

As I was paying for my petrol, the woman asked another customer if she had anything to spare and this person gave her some money. I walked to my car, shaking my head at what I thought was a waste of money. Then, I saw the stranger open her car door to reveal two smiling children, grateful to receive a meal. The woman had used the money to buy food for her children.

I realised that I had just experienced something very similar to the colt owner in today's scripture. The person I saw as a stranger and a nuisance was someone in need. I left, determined to remember that when we help to meet the needs of people around us, we serve Christ.

Prayer: *Dear God, open our eyes and show us that the needs of your people are your needs, too. Help us to continue to serve you by serving others in your name. Amen*

Thought for the day: Who is the Lord calling me to help today?

Jonathan Redding (Tennessee, US)

The Choice is Ours

Read Romans 5:1–5
We know that in all things God works for the good of those who love him, who have been called according to his purpose.
Romans 8:28 (NIV)

Recently our daughter Julie's doctors diagnosed her with an aggressive type of brain cancer, and they expect that she has only two years left to live. Despite this difficult diagnosis, Julie has decided to put her faith and confidence in God's word. (See her meditation on the next page.) Each morning and evening she listens to Bible passages and meditates on them throughout the day and night. She has decided to stay positive and to trust God to love and guide her throughout her life. Several people have expressed surprise at her attitude, but Julie knows that God is taking good care of her.

Life is filled with surprises, uncertainties and challenges. How we respond is our choice. We can become angry or bitter or we can choose to trust the promises of our loving, heavenly Father. We don't know what's ahead for Julie, but we do know that no matter what the future brings, God is present with her and with each of us.

Prayer: *Thank you, God, that we can trust you in every situation and circumstance. We don't know the future, but we do know that your love never ends. Thank you for your promises that give us peace and hope. Amen*

Thought for the day: I can trust God in every situation.

Donna Eliason (Washington, US)

Cancer Changed My Life

Read Isaiah 40:28–31

Those who hope in the Lord will renew their strength. They will soar on wings like eagles; they will run and not grow weary, they will walk and not be faint.

Isaiah 40:31 (NIV)

When I was diagnosed with brain cancer in March 2014, my life, dreams and goals changed instantly. The doctor said that after seeing my X-rays, he'd expected me to enter his surgery on a stretcher. However, as God enables me, I am fighting this cancer.

One way is by relying on God's promises. As I was raised in a Christian home, God's word permeates my mind. Every morning, my mum and I read scripture and pray. I have a very supportive family and know that people around the world are praying for me.

Even so, I have to be careful about my thoughts. Feelings of despair, discouragement and defeat come easily; but I can't dwell on them. Sometimes, when I get a report that my cancer is growing, I want to give up, but I know I can't. I resolve to trust God whatever happens, since I know that the Lord not only loves me but knows what I'm going through. God has plans for my life. It means a lot to me to remember that the Lord is here with me in every moment.

During these times, I remember stories of people who had to rely totally on God. I'd be terrified if I were to face lions (Daniel 6) or be thrown into a fiery furnace (Daniel 3). Yet I don't read about these men trying to escape. They trusted in the Lord's love and protection. Examples such as theirs help me to stand firm. I don't know how my story will end, but I do know I will continue to fight with everything I have and to trust in my Lord and Saviour every step of the way.

Prayer: *Dear God, thank you for giving us strength to endure hard times.*

Thought for the day: I can be encouraged by other people of faith.

Julie Douglas (Washington, US)

The Light of the World

Read John 1:1–5
When Jesus spoke again to the people, he said, 'I am the light of the world. Whoever follows me will never walk in darkness, but will have the light of life.'
John 8:12 (NIV)

For our service, our minister arranged tables in the form of a huge cross. Loaves of bread and chalices of wine, along with several candles, were on the tables. We sat around the cross and, during Communion, passed the bread and wine from person to person, serving each other. After Communion, several scripture passages were read. When each reading concluded, a candle was extinguished with a brass snuffer.

As I watched the tiny cup being lowered over the flame, cutting off its flow of oxygen, I was gripped by a powerful spiritual awareness. If we are to be lights for Christ in the world, we must have a source of life-giving spiritual energy. Without constant renewal by God's Spirit our light dims.

Our spiritual renewal comes through sharing in worship—praying, reading scripture and singing great hymns—fellowship with other Christians and acts of love and service. When we accept the grace offered in each of these practices, we will burn brightly and not burn out.

Prayer: *God of life and light, renew us by the power and presence of your Holy Spirit. May our lives shine with your love. Amen*

Thought for the day: God's life-giving light of love will brighten any darkness.

Everard Blackman (Queensland, Australia)

Abide In Me

Read John 6:53–57
Those who eat my flesh and drink my blood abide in me, and I in them.
John 6:56 (NRSV)

On the night before Jesus was crucified, he washed the disciples' feet and broke bread with them. He knew that his followers would face difficult days ahead, so he instructed them, 'Abide in me, and I in you' (John 15:4). The word 'abide' caught my eye. I longed to know what Jesus meant.

It occurred to me that one way Jesus explained this to the disciples was when he said that the wine they drank was his blood and the bread they ate was his body. If they drank the wine and ate the bread, then Jesus would be inside them and abide in them. Then, I flipped back through the Gospels, and I saw that when Jesus studied scripture, worshipped and prayed, he showed us some of the ways we can abide in him.

Abiding in Jesus offers us spiritual strength. As I thought about the times in my life when I was spiritually weak, I realised that they almost always coincided with times when I was not faithfully abiding in Jesus.

Each day, we have the opportunity to obey Jesus' instructions to abide in him. Communion, regular Bible reading, prayer and worship are more than healthy spiritual habits; they are an invitation to abide in Christ as he abides in us.

Prayer: *Dear God, help us to abide in Jesus Christ so that he may be part of all we think, say and do. Amen*

Thought for the day: How are you inviting Jesus to be part of your life?

Vicki Hines (Tennessee, US)

The Big One

Read Romans 8:1–11

Let us… approach the throne of grace with boldness, so that we may receive mercy and find grace to help in time of need.
Hebrews 4:16 (NRSV)

The powerful 1989 Loma Prieta earthquake sent buildings—and the upper level of the Nimitz motorway—crashing down. Sixty-three people died, and life around the San Francisco Bay area instantly slowed to a stunned, painful crawl as survivors rebuilt their lives. My colleagues and I remained on edge for months. Every aftershock set our hearts racing and our anxious minds anticipating the dreaded 'Big One' that scientists often warn us about. A friend described her reaction when the quake came: 'I prayed, "I'm sorry, God!"' In mortal danger—and not knowing God's grace—she immediately feared judgement.

God's judgement for our sins can be more frightening than any earthquake. Yet he does not want to punish us. His Son, Jesus Christ, stopped the crushing blow of judgement by dying on a Roman cross centuries ago; and God raised him from death. Like a strong building that stands firm through an earthquake, Christ's sacrifice protects us from the eternal consequences of sin. No matter what crisis or tragedy we may face, we know that the most important Big One has been neutralised. Rather than condemnation, through Christ we can feel peace and joy—in this life and in the life to come.

Prayer: *Steadfast God, when life's events frighten us, remind us that we can rest safe in your grace. Amen*

Thought for the day: Today and every day, God's love and grace will sustain me.

Columba Lisa Smith (California, US)

'Saturday'

Read Luke 23:44–56

It was the day of Preparation, and the sabbath was beginning. The women who had come with [Jesus] from Galilee followed, and they saw the tomb and how his body was laid.

Luke 23:54–55 (NRSV)

Jesus' followers were devastated by what had happened on Good Friday. They felt defeated and bewildered, wondering if they would meet a similar fate.

When our daughter was an adolescent, she drew a cartoon of Jesus sitting in the tomb before the large stone had been removed. He was looking at a wristwatch and thinking, 'Any minute now...'. The caption read, 'Saturday'. Although that seems like an innocent view of the crucified Christ, it described the anticipation I feel just before Easter. Those of us who know the rest of the story can look forward to the joy and celebration of the resurrection. Yet we may not appreciate the grief and futility that Jesus' followers experienced on Saturday because we already know what happens next.

The period beginning with Good Friday and ending on Easter Sunday morning is an especially appropriate time for fasting. Denying ourselves, reflecting on Jesus' sacrifice, praying, waiting—these disciplines prepare us for the joy of Easter. As we claim the resurrection for ourselves, so we share in the sorrow and grief that precedes it. Without experiencing the darkness, we cannot fully appreciate the light.

Prayer: *Father God, help us to dare to dwell in the darkness of the tomb today, so that we can experience the full joy of Easter morning.*

Thought for the day: Experiencing the darkness of sin and grief helps me appreciate the light of Jesus Christ.

David Turner (Texas, US)

Easter

Read Galatians 2:15–20

If the Spirit of him who raised Jesus from the dead is living in you, he who raised Christ from the dead will also give life to your mortal bodies because of his Spirit who lives in you.
Romans 8:11 (NIV)

I was spiritually dead and didn't know it. I grew up in a religious family and went to church every week. I attended church schools from primary school to college and thought I was living a good Christian life. Although I loved working in the church—and ended up becoming pastor of a large church—my heart was stone cold and legalistic. My relationship with my wife was unloving and lifeless. I needed help. Ironically, help came in the form of losing my pastoral position.

Over the next few years, after my old life had died, God replaced it by forging a new 'resurrected' personal relationship between us. In a sense, he rescued me by 'killing' my old life of perfectionism and replacing it with a life of hope, restored relationship with my wife and new ministry. Today I am truly that 'new creation' that Paul writes about (see 2 Corinthians 5:17).

When Jesus was crucified, the disciples believed that all was lost, but when he rose from the dead, everything changed. When life seems to be at its darkest point, we can turn to God and experience a resurrection to new life. God can continue to transform our relationships, health, finances, purpose and dreams. Easter isn't just a time to celebrate Jesus' resurrection 2000 years ago. It is a time to celebrate what God is doing in us every day—giving us new life.

Prayer: *Dear Jesus, remind us of the power in your shed blood and resurrection. Thank you for overcoming death and bringing us new life.*

Thought for the day: In Christ, I am a new creation (see 2 Corinthians 5:17).

Chad McComas (Oregon, US)

Our Constant God

Read Psalm 33:1–11

Jesus Christ is the same yesterday and today and for ever.

Hebrews 13:8 (NIV)

Grace is a remarkable woman who has an extremely good memory and can recall dates and names better than her younger friends. At a party for Grace, who was 92 at the time, people began to reminisce. 'Do you remember?' 'What about so and so?' 'Have you heard?' The conversations ranged to and fro, drawing forth many a smile.

Then Grace recalled how worship had changed. The form of music was different then; we heard none of the worship bands we have now. The hymns we sing today are different. Now we have more freedom and the dress is more casual.

The conversation made me realise that in spite of changes in our lives, God has not changed at all. He still forgives and comforts us, and requires repentance, acceptance and obedience from us. And his love remains constant.

Centuries may come and go; governments and nations rise and fall; people are born, live and die. God is, was and always will be.

Prayer: *Eternal God, help us to dedicate ourselves to you in each stage of life. Amen*

Thought for the day: All else may change, but God remains the same.

Carol Purves (Cumbria, England)

In Sync

Read Ephesians 4:2–6

Be filled with the Spirit, speaking to one another with psalms, hymns and songs from the Spirit. Sing and make music from your heart to the Lord.
Ephesians 5:18–19 (NIV)

As my son and the other school band members played at their concert, I enjoyed the music. But at the grand finale, several students played too fast while others lagged behind. The song became noisy and disjointed. The conductor signalled for them to stop. She tapped the baton on her music stand and announced, 'From 52!' Finding the bar number in their scores, watching her and then listening to each other this time, the children finished the song as one.

Similarly, we are often out of sync when making decisions in church. Though we've made a common commitment to Christ, we don't always think and plan alike. When we allow pride, ego and envy to create discord, noisy dissonance is the result. But I've found that during those times when our visions for the church don't align, we can find harmony once again if we follow the lead of the Holy Spirit and accept others with humility and gentleness.

In our communities of faith, conflicts will come up and we may fall out of sync along the way. When that happens, we can pay attention to the guidance of our patient and loving Conductor. We can listen to one another and pick up where we left off, going forward with unity through the bond of peace (see Ephesians 4:3).

Prayer: *Peace-loving Father, in times of conflict, show us how to be in sync with your Spirit. Amen*

Thought for the day: How can I stay in sync with the Holy Spirit in times of conflict?

Lynn Hare (Oregon, US)

Who's My Neighbour?

Read Luke 10:25–37
Love your neighbour as yourself.
Luke 10:27 (NIV)

My wife and I were driving back home from California, hurrying to meet an appointment. When we stopped for petrol, a young woman approached me and told me that her family was stranded and needed help. The last thing I wanted to deal with was anything that would cause us further delay. I told her that I was sorry but I couldn't help her.

When we were back on the road, the scene with the woman kept playing in my mind. She had asked for help, and I had turned her down. I said a silent prayer that God would provide the woman and her family with assistance and comfort in their time of need. I also reflected on my own failure to help them, adding a request for forgiveness for selfishly putting my own needs above those of her family.

Jesus lived a life of sacrifice and compassion, and he calls us to do the same. Today's reading from Luke demonstrates what it means to be a good neighbour. Unfortunately, I had behaved in the same manner as the priest and the Levite in today's reading, ignoring a neighbour in need. But while I fell short that time, it strengthened my resolve to be more sensitive in the future, and to be the good neighbour that Christ calls us to be.

Prayer: *Forgive us, O God, when we fail to care for those who need our help. Strengthen us for the task of being a good neighbour. Amen*

Thought for the day: When we serve others, we are serving Christ.

John D. Bown (Minnesota, US)

What to Do?

Read James 5:13–16

Devote yourselves to prayer, being watchful and thankful.
Colossians 4:2 (NIV)

Late one afternoon my eye doctor dilated my pupils for a routine check-up, and everything looked blurry. For several hours after I returned home I could not cook, read, crochet, watch TV or enjoy my other usual activities. I wondered how I would spend the time.

Amid my frustration with this temporary inconvenience, I suddenly realised, 'I can pray.' Then I spent an evening praising God and interceding for family members, friends and my church fellowship.

Isn't prayer what God has always desired from us? Consider Noah making a new beginning (Genesis 8:13–20), King Jehoshaphat facing a huge invading army (2 Chronicles 20:1–28), or the church at Jerusalem hearing of Peter's imprisonment (Acts 12:1–17). Whatever we are facing, God calls us to pray.

Prayer: *Gracious God, help us to turn to you in all circumstances. Thank you for the privilege of prayer. As Jesus taught us, we pray, 'Our Father which art in heaven, Hallowed be thy name. Thy kingdom come. Thy will be done in earth, as it is in heaven. Give us this day our daily bread. And forgive us our debts, as we forgive our debtors. And lead us not into temptation, but deliver us from evil: For thine is the kingdom, and the power, and the glory, for ever. Amen.'**

Thought for the day: I can always pray.

Linda P. Hamilton (Colorado, US)

* Matthew 6:9–13 (KJV)

The Rock Redeemed

Read Luke 22:54–62

In [Jesus Christ] we have redemption through his blood, the forgiveness of sins, in accordance with the riches of God's grace.
Ephesians 1:7 (NIV)

One of the most emotional passages in the Gospels describes Peter's denial of Christ. Following Jesus' arrest, Peter—the man Jesus had proclaimed would be the rock upon which he would build his church (see Matthew 16:18)—three times denied any knowledge of our Lord. But rather than being appalled by Peter's actions, my heart goes out to him. It's easy for me to imagine the fear he must have felt and to identify with his shame.

We've all been faced with the dilemma of knowing we should stand up for what's right but being too afraid to do so. Regret always follows. If Peter's story ended there, it would be a very tragic one. But Jesus knew all that would happen that day (Luke 22:34), and he had already forgiven his disciple. Peter would go on to become the rock that Jesus said he would be. He played a vital role in the early days of a movement that would ultimately lead untold millions to salvation through Christ.

Peter's story is one of fear, shame and, ultimately, redemption. That's not the outcome we might expect. But it's a perfect illustration of the truth that with God's grace, all things are possible.

Prayer: *Dear God, thank you for helping us to overcome our fears, set aside shame and embrace the salvation made available to us by the grace of your Son. Amen*

Thought for the day: Everyone who seeks God can be redeemed.

Dan Busha (Florida, US)

Foundation on the Rock

Read Luke 6:47–49

Someone… who comes to me, hears my words, and acts on them… is like a man building a house, who dug deeply and laid the foundation on rock; when a flood arose, the river burst against that house but could not shake it, because it had been well built.

Luke 6:47–48 (NRSV)

Walking along the lake shore, I looked to the path above. Earlier, while on that path, I had seen signs warning hikers to keep back from the edge, though everything had looked fine. Trees were still growing along the path. But from below, I could see that the winter storms had ravaged the bank and in many places had left an overhang with no foundation to support it. When I saw roots dangling free beneath a thin layer of soil, I knew that the trees would not survive for long. Without a solid foundation to anchor them, they could come crashing down at any minute.

This scene was a vivid reminder of what life would be like without the firm foundation that God provides. From the outside our lives may look fine. But the sorrow of loss, the pain of illness or the hurt of rejection can shake us. In Philippians 4:13 the apostle Paul wrote, 'I can do all things through [Christ] who strengthens me.' By spending time reading the Bible and talking with God in prayer, we build the firm foundation that can keep us secure through life's storms.

Prayer: *Thank you, Lord Jesus, for providing the firm foundation that we need to remain strong amid the storms of life. Amen*

Thought for the day: God gives me strength to handle today's storms.

Tandy Balson (Alberta, Canada)

To the Rescue

Read Psalm 142:1–7

Learn to do good; seek justice, rescue the oppressed, defend the orphan, plead for the widow.
Isaiah 1:17 (NRSV)

I remember an upsetting incident from my childhood. Hearing a great cacophony of chirping on the lawn, I discovered that a flock of sparrows had surrounded an albino sparrow. Ferociously, they pecked at the unusual bird, screeching and hemming him in. The birds on the edge of the group flapped about—waiting their turn to attack—as the albino crouched, helpless. I ran clapping my hands and yelling, 'Stop that!' The brown sparrows flew away, twittering among themselves. The albino hesitated for a moment, dazed and injured, then flew to the nearest bush.

That experience made an impression on me because I had witnessed bullying in school. Back then, adults often shrugged off rude words or aggressive behaviour as 'kids just being kids'. But these days, people take hurtful words and actions that can affect children for a lifetime seriously. Jesus calls us not to be bystanders when others are being mistreated but instead to be active in making our world kinder. The psalmist cried to God when others made him suffer. Today, we can help answer cries like his as we follow God's call to prevent cruelty and display compassion.

Prayer: *Thank you, Lord, for your love. May we have the courage to share it with others—especially those who are oppressed. Amen*

Thought for the day: When someone is being mistreated, God calls me into action.

Genie Stoker (Arizona, US)

How to Move a Mountain

Read Matthew 17:14–21

Jesus said, 'If you have faith the size of a mustard seed, you will say to this mountain, "Move from here to there", and it will move; and nothing will be impossible for you.'

Matthew 17:20 (NRSV)

A church I know of needed a high mound behind the building moved so that they could use the space as a car park. The pastor declared a 'Move-the-Mountain Sunday', a concerted effort of prayer during the morning service. Alas, on Monday morning, the mound of earth was still there. However, also there, at the church door, stood an official from the highway department. 'We need thousands of tons of earth for a road project,' he told the church staff. 'We were wondering if we could remove part of the mound from behind your church.'

The moral of the story is that God will help us do what we can do. In scripture, we see God and humans cooperating to perform miracles. When Jesus raised Lazarus from the dead, he asked the bystanders first to move the rock sealing the tomb and then to help Lazarus take off his grave clothes (John 11:39, 44). In Mark 2:1–5, the friends of a lame man couldn't heal him, but they did what they could do: they removed part of the roof and lowered him in front of Jesus. When Jesus multiplied loaves and fishes, the disciples distributed the food and collected the leftovers (Matthew 14:19–21).

Each of us will face a mountain at some time or another. In these times, rather than moving a mountain for us, God may provide a shovel—or the highway department!

Prayer: *Dear God of miracles, show us what part we can play for you to 'move mountains' in our lives. Amen*

Thought for the day: What tools has God provided me today to help move a mountain?

James N. Watkins (Indiana, US)

Gifts and Talents

Read Psalm 90:9–12
This is the gift of God: that all people should eat, drink, and enjoy the results of their hard work.
Ecclesiastes 3:13 (CEB)

When I was young, I enrolled in a technical college. From the subjects available, I chose dressmaking, opting for fashion design. This skill came very naturally to me, and I believed that it was a God-given talent. Ever since, I have enjoyed designing and creating, even though I decided not to turn my skill into a business. Instead, I devoted my time to serving my friends and family. As I worked on sewing projects for them, I developed a form of prayer discipline. Each project I undertook was an opportunity to have a dialogue with God. I would ask him to guide me with wisdom; as my hands worked, my heart prayed.

The years have gone by quickly. Now my life is not quite as fast-paced, my vision is not what it used to be and my hands are not quite as steady. However, I am still in constant communication with my Creator in every activity I undertake. I am grateful for the opportunity to work with God by my side. I am blessed that even in my frailty, he is my constant companion.

Prayer: *Gracious God, thank you for the gifts and talents you have bestowed. Help us to use them in your service. Amen*

Thought for the day: Today I will communicate with God while using my talents.

Mabel Muñoz de Varas (Arica y Parinacota, Chile)

What Else Is There?

Read Mark 9:14–29

[The Lord] said to me, 'My grace is sufficient for you, for power is made perfect in weakness.' So, I will boast all the more gladly of my weaknesses, so that the power of Christ may dwell in me.
2 Corinthians 12:9 (NRSV)

We lost our only son to suicide; our daughter lost her only sibling. Even though we have had other losses, this has been the most devastating loss we have experienced as a family. My daughter asked me recently if my faith in God has held. Is my faith enough? I thought about this for a long time. My faith had surely been tested, and I had had times of despair, doubt, sorrow and even anger. I had read scripture, prayed more than ever before, attended church, participated in a grief group and received comfort from friends. Still, I was not yet able to answer her question. I mentioned the conversation to a friend, who said, 'But what else is there? What is the alternative to faith?' My friend's response went to the heart of the question. I had my answer. Yes, my faith is holding. The grace Jesus offers is sufficient.

My faith may not be as strong as I would like it to be, and I have more questions than answers about my son's death. I do believe my faith will see me through my earthly life. Nothing is better than my holding to my faith in Jesus Christ. 'I believe; help my unbelief!' (Mark 9:24).

Prayer: *May we never abandon our faith, Lord, because we know you will never abandon us. Help us to hold on to your promises of hope and eternity. Amen*

Thought for the day: God is always with us—whatever our circumstances.

Mary J. Penny (Alabama, US)

God's Blueprints

Read Luke 14:28–30
Unless the Lord builds the house, those who build it labour in vain.
Psalm 127:1 (NRSV)

When I was at high school I took classes in architectural drawing because I wanted to build shimmering towers like those in my hometown of Houston, Texas. But instead of being inspired to design something big and grand, I was instructed to draw letters of the alphabet and a metal bolt. I got bored fast! Even though I didn't pursue architecture as a career, I still feel the desire to build and create. But my dreaming has led me down some pretty bumpy roads: business with an unethical partner, money lost on risky ideas, trying to launch a cutting-edge ministry without proper organisation and support.

About the time I realised that my latest venture was going nowhere, I came across Psalm 127. I became painfully aware that too often I fail to discern if my plans are God's plans. We can listen for his instructions by studying the Bible—our Creator's blueprint for living—and then take action as the Spirit guides us. Now when I have a plan, I write down all the steps and details, pray about each of them and alter any that do not reflect the values and principles laid out in scripture. Only when we have put our plans completely into God's hands can we glorify him in what we accomplish.

Prayer: *Father God, help us to know and remain focused on your designs for building our lives in ways that are pleasing to you. Amen*

Thought for the day: How do I seek God's guidance when I am making plans?

Kenneth Avon White (Tennessee, US)

God's Generosity

Read Matthew 20:1–16

[Give] joyful thanks to the Father, who has qualified you to share in the inheritance of his holy people in the kingdom of light.
Colossians 1:12 (NIV)

I was shocked and saddened to hear last year of my cousin's sudden death at the age of 64. I was even more shocked when I found out I was named among a group of five people to each receive a small inheritance. I could understand why the two friends would be included in his will; they had been close friends for decades. And the two other cousins had a much closer relationship with him; they did more to help him when he was ill. I hadn't had the same type of relationship and I felt unworthy of such a gift. Why did he choose me, not only to receive his gift, but to have an equal share in it? When I questioned the executor of the will I was told that my cousin had loved me and wanted me to have a share.

I see a reminder of Christ's relationship with humans. God loves us and sent Jesus to die so that we can receive salvation. Our inheritance isn't determined by how long we have travelled with Christ. Even when we feel as if we don't deserve it, we are all entitled to equal shares in God's kingdom.

Prayer: *Loving God, it's hard to accept that we don't have to be worthy to receive an equal share in the kingdom. Thank you for your life so freely given. Amen*

Thought for the day: I have an equal share in God's amazing love.

Lenore Warton (New South Wales, Australia)

Small Expressions

Read Luke 17:11–19

Thanks be to God for his indescribable gift!
2 Corinthians 9:15 (NRSV)

I had never formed the habit of saying grace before meals. I had always just assumed that if I could earn the money to buy food, why should I thank anyone else for it? But after a series of physical and financial setbacks I began to be more grateful for what I had. My wife and I now give thanks before each meal, as a sign of gratitude for the ways God has blessed us.

One day in a local restaurant after finishing our meal, I felt a hand on my shoulder. Looking up, I saw a man smiling at me. He said, 'It's so refreshing to see someone giving thanks to God, when so many others just take what they have for granted.' Even small expressions of gratitude can have a powerful effect. It doesn't take a lot of effort. For all God gives us and for the example we show others when we express our appreciation for his gifts, giving thanks is truly worth the time.

Prayer: *Dear Lord, let us never forget that you are the source of our every blessing. We pray as Jesus taught us, saying, 'Our Father which art in heaven, Hallowed be thy name. Thy kingdom come. Thy will be done, as in heaven, so in earth. Give us day by day our daily bread. And forgive us our sins; for we also forgive every one that is indebted to us. And lead us not into temptation; but deliver us from evil. Amen.'**

Thought for the day: Saying 'thank you' to God is never a wasted effort.

Mark A. Carter (Texas, US)

* Luke 11:2–4 (KJV)

Listening

Read Psalm 81:8–16

The Lord says, 'If my people would only listen to me, if Israel would only follow my ways, how quickly I would subdue their enemies and turn my hand against their foes!'

Psalm 81:13–14 (NIV)

One day, when my husband and I were arguing, he said, 'Sweetheart, you are always right, but you don't listen to me.' That was a wake-up call for me. All the advice on successful marriage emphasises communication skills—especially the importance of listening. As I reflected on this, I discovered that the reason I did not listen was because I was focused on myself. My pride wanted to prove that I was right and that my husband was wrong. I needed to learn to put myself in my husband's shoes and listen to his point of view. After all, the Bible teaches us to 'be quick to listen, slow to speak' (James 1:19).

Listening is also important in our prayer lives. If prayer is conversation with God, then we will listen to what he is saying to us. It may well be that when we listen to and obey God, he will do for us as he promised Israel—to subdue any forces that are hindering us. So the next time we pray, we can focus on God, not on ourselves and our circumstances. Our prayers may not always produce the answers we seek, but our lives can be transformed by listening to and obeying him.

Prayer: *Almighty God, help us to listen to your voice with our hearts, our minds, and our spirits. Amen*

Thought for the day: Listening is an expression of love for God.

Tracy Hsu Jensen (California, US)

How Long Will You Grieve?

Read 1 Samuel 16:1–13

The Lord said to Samuel, 'How long will you grieve over Saul?... Fill your horn with oil and set out; I will send you to Jesse the Bethlehemite, for I have provided for myself a king among his sons.'
1 Samuel 16:1 (NRSV)

Following God's instructions, Samuel anointed Saul to be king over Israel (see 1 Samuel 15:1). Later, Samuel grieved over Saul's failure to obey God. But God needed Samuel to do his part to anoint a new king. He instructed Samuel to go to Bethlehem to anoint one of Jesse's sons. Samuel protested (see 1 Samuel 16:2) when God asked him, 'How long will you grieve over Saul?'

Like Samuel, we are often unable to move on with life after deep disappointments—the break-up of a marriage, the death or injury of a loved one, or the loss of a job and financial stability. We are so busy grieving over what was or what will never be that we are unable to see the new direction God has for us. God does not judge by the outward appearance of people, but rather by the heart, and he sees to the heart of human life. We may not find happiness in the way the world defines it. But when we truly surrender to God, our greatest desire is to serve him. In the midst of our deepest disappointments and defeat, he is not finished with us. How long will we grieve? God is ready to help us move forward.

Prayer: *God of hope, help us when we grieve over what has been or what will never be. Thank you for giving us the strength to continue even when we feel defeated. Amen*

Thought for the day: God is waiting for me with the strength to help me move forward.

Michael Macdonald (North Carolina, US)

Being Prepared

Read Psalm 119:97–105
You are my refuge and my shield; I have put my hope in your word.
Psalm 119:114 (NIV)

What began as an ordinary meal with a friend changed the instant Laura began choking on her dinner. Sitting across the table, Elin knew she had only seconds to respond. Jumping to her feet and praying, 'Lord, let this work', she wrapped her arms around Laura and began applying the Heimlich manoeuvre. Three abdominal thrusts later, the food dislodged from Laura's throat. Elin's experience demonstrated the benefit of preparation. In that moment, a technique she learned many years ago and had never before needed helped to save her friend's life.

I've noticed the same principle at work in my spiritual life. Biblical truths I learned long ago become essential in today's times of crisis. Passages that seemed boring suddenly come to life when I'm faced with a similar circumstance. If I hadn't taken the time to learn those truths, the wisdom wouldn't have been within me when I needed it. Experiences such as Elin's motivate me to engage in regular Bible study with others. Then, in the midst of a trial, the Spirit brings to mind what I've learned and provides the help I need. Just as Elin had to learn the Heimlich manoeuvre to be prepared for a moment of crisis, I need to prepare so that I can face whatever potentially destructive circumstances enter my life.

Prayer: *Dear Father, help us to read your word faithfully each day, so we will be prepared for the trials life brings. Amen*

Thought for the day: God's word provides tools for living.

Lynn Karidis (Michigan, US)

Stop, Look and Share

Read Luke 24:13–35

To you has been given the secret of the kingdom of God, but for those outside, everything comes in parables; in order that 'they may indeed look, but not perceive, and may indeed listen, but not understand'.
Mark 4:11–12 (NRSV)

We were in a hurry to catch the bus. 'But stop, Daddy,' said my daughter as she bent down to look at the caterpillar at her feet. She picked it up, marvelled at its hairy-looking body, and chuckled at the number of feet. Only after she had carefully placed the caterpillar somewhere safe, where no one would step on it, did we continue on our journey.

My daughter's curiosity offered me a fresh insight that morning. In today's reading, Jesus offered the two companions a new understanding. After they had spoken with Jesus, they saw things from a new perspective—a divine point of view. How often do we need others to point things out to us that we cannot see for ourselves? But that's not the end of the story in Luke 24. Just like my daughter who had to share her discovery of the caterpillar with me, Cleopas and his companion could not keep this discovery to themselves but had to share it.

Prayer: *Dear Lord Jesus, help us to be open to the new insights you offer us, from wherever and whomever they come. Amen*

Thought for the day: Today I will look for God in nature.

Ken Kingston (Buckinghamshire, England)

The Power of Touch

Read John 20:19–31

[Jesus] said to Thomas, 'Put your finger here and see my hands. Reach out your hand and put it in my side. Do not doubt but believe.'
John 20:27 (NRSV)

Because I am blind, touch is important to me. I use Braille to read the Bible and the notes I have prepared to teach my Sunday school class. Friends will describe the floral arrangements on our church altar, but I need to touch the flowers fully to appreciate their beauty. For me, a warm handshake or hug is an especially important connection with someone. The sun on my skin or the gentle breeze in my hair reminds me that God is creating new life. Perhaps this is why I am drawn to the story of Thomas and his need to touch the risen Jesus. Thomas was absent when Jesus appeared to the disciples inside the locked room the first time. And I often wonder, 'Where was he? Had his grief led him to wander alone? Why did he isolate himself from those who shared his suffering? Was he afraid of being identified with the followers of Jesus?'

We are not given answers to these questions, but we are told that one week later Jesus returned and this time Thomas was present. Jesus told Thomas to touch the wounds left by crucifixion. He wanted to do whatever it took to help Thomas believe he was alive and real. Jesus seeks to reveal himself in unique ways to each of us.

Prayer: *Loving God, awaken all my senses to your living presence. Amen*

Thought for the day: How is Jesus revealing himself to me today?

Karen E. Brown (Mississippi, US)

A Tree of Life

Read Ephesians 2:4–10

We are God's handiwork, created in Christ Jesus to do good works, which God prepared in advance for us to do.
Ephesians 2:10 (NIV)

At the edge of the field near my home stands a tree that has been struck by lightning several times. It is a splintered mass of scorched wood and pulp that is discoloured from disease. Some of its wounds are recent, but some are partially grown over—this tree has been a real survivor. It is not only still alive, but out of a diseased and blackened scar a few feet from the ground, a large branch has continued to grow. In the early spring, this scarred and deformed tree is covered with light green buds, and within its branches is nestled a bird's nest. If you only saw the base of the tree, you'd see a shattered, disease-ridden stump. If you only saw the branch jutting out, you'd think you were looking at a healthy tree. In both cases you would be mistaken about the tree's true condition, and in neither case would you be seeing the tree for what it really is: one of God's many miracles.

When we encounter someone scarred by a traumatic event or weathered by long-term disease or disability, we might make incorrect assumptions based on what we see. But that person has the potential to grow, thrive, bloom and nurture others. Each person is made in the image of God and is another one of his many miracles.

Prayer: *Dear God, please help us to remember that every person is your child, created in your image. Amen*

Thought for the day: Each person I meet is created in God's image.

Rebecca Canfield (Maryland, US)

PRAYER FOCUS: SOMEONE I HAVE JUDGED WRONGLY   115

Higher Ground

Read Isaiah 40:1–5

I lift up my eyes to the mountains—where does my help come from? My help comes from the Lord, the Maker of heaven and earth.
Psalm 121:1–2 (NIV)

I was driving when I looked up and saw the hills ahead of me. They seemed very tall. Then I drove on, my thoughts on other things and the hills forgotten. A few minutes later I looked up again and was surprised to see that the hills ahead weren't nearly as high as I had thought. 'What happened to those hills?' I asked myself. Then I realised that without my noticing it, the road had been climbing upward. I was now on higher ground.

So often my problems can be like those hills. They can seem large and insurmountable from the valley of my own perspective. However, when I spend time praising and worshipping God and bring my problems to him in prayer, then I move to higher ground. The problems no longer seem huge and insurmountable. From a perspective shaped by God, they have become something he and I can easily cope with together. I need constantly to make the decision to shift my focus from myself and the burdens of life to God. On higher ground with him, although all things are not easy, all things are possible.

Prayer: *Father God, help us to focus on you each day so that we can see things from a spiritual perspective and know that with you all things are possible. Amen*

Thought for the day: I can decide to make God the focus of my life.

Ann Stewart (South Australia, Australia)

Springing Back

Read 1 Peter 1: 3–9

The Lord is good, a refuge in times of trouble. He cares for those who trust in him.
Nahum 1:7 (NIV)

My job at a plant nursery involves propagating trees. Taking a small bud from one variety of tree, we graft it onto the root stock of another variety. In time, the two develop as one—growing tall and seemingly strong—but the process does not end there. When the tree has matured, we check it by using the simple test of pushing against the trunk. If the graft has properly healed, the tree will bend with the pressure and spring back when released. If the graft has not healed, the tree may still look healthy. When force is applied, however, hidden weakness is exposed and the trunk will snap off at the graft.

So it is when pressures push in on us and our faith is tested. If our spiritual life has little depth, all may look well; but like the tree, we may easily break under stress. Spending time in God's presence through prayer and daily reading of scripture prepares and strengthens us for times of trouble. In the midst of trial, we can call on what we have learned about the Lord in those quiet moments. In Jesus—the strong vine from which we as branches grow (see John 15:5)—we may bend, but we won't break.

Prayer: *Dear Lord, strengthen us through your grace in order that we may face our trials with the confidence that you are with us every step of the way. Amen*

Thought for the day: My strength comes from my relationship with Jesus.

Steven C. Beebe (Washington, US)

The Soldier

Read Psalm 144: 1–15
'Your kingdom come, your will be done, on earth as it is in heaven.'
Matthew 6:10 (NIV)

Watching my son line up with his regiment, I stood, lost in memories. I remembered tucking him into bed with his teddy bear. I thought about his running to hug me so tightly that I could not breathe. His mischievous grin lit up a room. Tears gathered in my eyes, but I held them in, struggling to be brave. I heard the sergeant call for attention, and the soldiers turned to march to the plane. 'I love you,' I whispered one more time. My heart cried out to God. I prayed that he would protect my son and that he would be open to know God. In my heart, I placed my son in God's care saying, 'Your will be done.'

I wanted to protect my son from the dangers of the war. I could not protect him, but I could trust God; I had released my son into his hands. As I did, I remembered the words of Psalm 144:2 'He is my loving God and my fortress, my stronghold and my deliverer, my shield in whom I take refuge.'

Whatever happens, I know God will be with us. We cannot control all the circumstances in our lives, but we can trust God to carry us through the darkness. Because his grace and mercy endure, he will never fail us.

Prayer: *Faithful God, may your will be done in our lives today, and may we trust you with all we have. Amen*

Thought for the day: In the storms of life, God reaches down to carry us.

L.F. Ward (Alabama, US)

Who Are You?

Read John 10:1–6

See, I have inscribed you on the palms of my hands.
Isaiah 49:16 (NRSV)

I have difficulty in recognising people's faces, including those of my friends I haven't seen for some time. This can be embarrassing. I met a former classmate one day in a street in Kuala Lumpur, Malaysia; but I did not recognise him, even though we had been good friends in school. I asked, 'Who are you?' Because he is kind, he responded graciously.

Remembering people is difficult for many of us but not for our great and faithful God. He never forgets us and knows each of us by name. Isaiah 45:3 says, 'I am the Lord, the God of Israel, who summons you by name' (NIV). John 10:3 tells about the good shepherd: 'He calls his own sheep by name.' God even knows the name of each star in heaven. 'He determines the number of the stars and calls them each by name,' says Psalm 147:4.

How much more will God know and remember his children on earth! We may worry that our friends will one day ask, 'Who are you?' However, we can rest assured that wherever we are and at any time, we can rely on God and our Lord Jesus Christ to remember us always. This is the promise of our Father in heaven.

Prayer: *Dear God, our heavenly Creator and Father, thank you for assurance that you know and recognise each of us always. Amen*

Thought for the day: God knows and recognises us always.

Kong Peng Sun (Singapore)

Grandad's Walking Stick

Read Psalm 23:1–6

Even though I walk through the darkest valley, I will fear no evil, for you are with me; your rod and your staff, they comfort me.
Psalm 23:4 (NIV)

In my bedroom wardrobe is a metal walking stick. It belonged to my grandad and then to my father. During my father's battle with cancer, he walked with slow measured steps while gripping grandad's walking stick. As the years pass, the day may come when it will help me to walk too.

The walking stick reminds me of scripture, the staff I lean on in my spiritual walk and especially during difficult times. When my father died, a staff of comfort to me was Psalm 68:5: 'A father to the fatherless… is God.' When I was emotionally and physically exhausted from dealing with my father's estate, 'I will refresh the weary and satisfy the faint' (Jeremiah 31:25) promised rest and renewal. And when a lump in my breast filled me with fear, I leaned on Matthew 9:22, 'Take heart, daughter; your faith has made you well' (NRSV), for hope and healing.

As we traverse our valleys of grief, doubt, fear and depression, we have a staff that reassures us that we are not walking alone: 'Surely I am with you always' (Matthew 28:20). Psalm 23 is a staff I lean on for comfort. It promises that whatever we are coping with, the Good Shepherd is with us for emotional and spiritual support.

Prayer: *Dear Lord, thank you for your staff that provides emotional comfort and spiritual support. Amen*

Thought for the day: God's staff steadies our steps through the darkest valleys.

Debra Pierce (Massachusetts, US)

God Is Love

Read 1 John 4:7–21

This is love: not that we loved God, but that God loved us and sent his Son as an atoning sacrifice for our sins.
1 John 4:10 (NIV)

Love has been defined in many different ways. One of those ways is that love is something we do. We love. We do. We make a difference. The apostle John saw it differently. Love, he says, is not primarily something we do, but something God does or is. Our love is responsive, reactive and reflexive to God's love. We can let go of the notion that love—or anything else—starts with us. It begins with God, who is the Alpha and Omega, the beginning and end, the first and last.

Here's the great news: We can relax, knowing that love doesn't originate with us, but comes from an endless, abounding, overflowing, incredible and amazing supply. We can draw on God's love and let it overflow to and through us. God's love may lead us to some surprising places and circumstances, but he will already be there. He sets an example of sacrificial love for us. Because God's love is sacrificial, we can expect to make some sacrifice as well. We love because he first loved us.

Prayer: *Dear God, teach us to love as you love, sacrificing our own desires for the good of others. Amen*

Thought for the day: 'God is love' (1 John 4:8).

Dan G. Johnson (Florida, US)

The Gold Standard

Read Job 23:1–10

The Lord says, 'A bruised reed he will not break, and a smouldering wick he will not snuff out. In faithfulness he will bring forth justice.'

Isaiah 42:3 (NIV)

The battle with cancer that was slowly taking my husband had the two of us on a rollercoaster of optimism and dashed hopes. I was so angry with God that I was ready to explode! In the midst of this terrible trial, I attended a Christian women's conference. As I sat with folded arms, determined not to listen, I heard the speaker ask, 'Have you ever been angry with God?' She had my attention. Then she read the Bible verse quoted above. I walked to my car thinking, 'God, this reed is about to snap. If any wick is smouldering, I can't see it.'

When I got home, I turned to Job 23. As I read each verse, I slapped the page angrily, until I came to verse 10: '[God] knows the way that I take; when he has tested me, I will come forth as gold.' I stopped. Knowing that gold is refined through exposure to tremendous heat that separates out the impurities, I saw a connection to my own situation. Suddenly, I became aware of the impurities within me—especially jealousy, resentment and self-pity. I knew that I needed to ask God for help and forgiveness, and, when I did, calm replaced anger and peace replaced fear.

In the weeks that followed, I continued to examine my attitudes and ask for forgiveness, and though God's words did not change my circumstances, they did change my heart. God does not say that a reed can't be bruised or that a candle can't burn low. But he has promised always to be present and faithful in giving us strength.

Prayer: *Lord, we do not understand suffering, but we do know that you take care of us. When we rail against you, replace our anger with trust.*

Thought for the day: In the heat of trouble, God's grace can purify.

Karen Weaver (Ohio, US)

Springtime Promise

Read Psalm 37:1–9

The Lord makes firm the steps of the one who delights in him; though he may stumble, he will not fall, for the Lord upholds him with his hand.
Psalm 37:23–24 (NIV)

I love spring. I love bright mornings with the promise of summer when gradually, day by day, buds form and leaves start to emerge on the trees. And when the weather at times turns cold and windy, I feel anxious that the buds might retreat and wait for better weather, as we might, before venturing out. But thankfully they don't, and I always marvel at their tenacious ability to keep budding and keep growing until they are fully formed, regardless of adversity and inclement conditions.

They remind me of our journey through life. We can follow God's word on sunny bright days when things are going well, but if we face adversity and storm clouds gather, do we run for cover, lose faith and retreat? In these situations we can try to be like the buds of spring, walking firmly onwards with Christ, our hand in his. Then we can face life's challenges full on, confident in his love and support at all times. Then, too, the brightness of his love may be reflected in and through us to others who need our help.

Prayer: *Lord, we thank you that we can be sure of your love and support at all times, that we can walk with our hand in yours. Help us to be willing to share that love with others, offering them our hands for support. Amen*

Thought for the day: Today I will share God's support with others.

Judy Wagner (Lothian, Scotland)

The Trust Factor

Read Nehemiah 1:1–11

[Nehemiah prayed] 'Lord, let your ear be attentive to the prayer of this your servant and to the prayer of your servants who delight in revering your name.'

Nehemiah 1:11 (NIV)

For years my journey to work has taken me under and over several motorway bridges. Sometimes, looking up at a bridge I was passing under, I would see half a dozen lorries, waiting there for the traffic lights to change. At other times, I would be driving over water on a bridge that I trusted to be strong enough for the weight of my car and all those around me. One day I found myself thinking that every day I trust these structures of concrete and steel to do their job. But do I trust God that much? What if I were to trust him more with my life and family?

In the Old Testament, Nehemiah is recorded as crying out to God to help him and his fellow conquered Israelites. They were all slaves, and their plight seemed hopeless. But Nehemiah persevered in talking to God. Again and again he acknowledged that the situation was far greater than he could handle and then asked God for help. From scripture, we know how much God cares about our circumstances and is willing and able to help us. Even though a situation may seem hopeless—a prodigal adult child, an incurable illness or a fear that doesn't seem to leave us alone—we can pray, confident that God hears us.

Prayer: *Dear God, whether we are facing a small crisis or a seemingly impossible task, remind us that you hear our prayers and answer them.*

Thought for the day: God cares about me even more than I can imagine.

Pamela Gilsenan (Colorado, US)

Clearer Vision

Read John 9:13–16, 35–41

Jesus said, 'I came into this world for judgement so that those who do not see may see, and those who do see may become blind.'
John 9:39 (NRSV)

One day, I accompanied my friend to an eye test. While there, I was asked if I wanted to undergo the same eye examination as my friend. I said I didn't think I needed glasses; I felt I could see well enough. However, I decided to go ahead with the examination, more out of curiosity than a sense of need. When the examination had finished, the optician explained that my vision was not good, that I should have begun using glasses years ago. He further explained that when people come in for appointments, they are often convinced their vision is fine because they have no point of reference. They are not aware of their poor vision until they look through graduated lenses and notice the difference.

After this experience, I reflected on our relationship with God. We believe that our relationship is fine—that is, until we have an experience of God's joy, peace, assurance and loving presence that deepens our relationship. We view things through a different lens and gain a new perspective—one that brings us into closer intimacy with God.

Prayer: *Loving God, we are grateful for the joy of knowing you. Help us to proclaim your word to those who do not know you. Amen*

Thought for the day: When I focus on God, I can be more open to the transforming love of my Creator.

Algae Loya (Chihuahua, Mexico)

God's Constant Love

Read 1 John 4:13–16
If anyone acknowledges that Jesus is the Son of God, God lives in them and they in God.
1 John 4:15 (NIV)

A few days ago I was looking at a series of photographs of sunrises and sunsets which I had taken in different parts of the world.

I realised afresh that the sun always rises in the morning and sets in the evening. No matter where we are in the world we can rely on those facts about the sun. It may be obscured at times by bad weather conditions, but it is still there. We can depend on it.

I was reminded that God is like that. No matter where we are or what happens to us, he will be there. He never changes. Sometimes we find it difficult to see him, especially when things are going badly, or when we wander away from him, but he is still there. He never deviates from his course or his plan for us. We can trust in that knowledge. We can depend on God and put our trust in his constant care for us. His glory is reflected in the world he created and in the lives of those who know him and serve him.

Prayer: *Lord, we give you thanks for your unfailing love and care for us. Help us always to trust you, in whatever circumstances we find ourselves. Amen*

Thought for the day: As the sun rises on a new day, I will remember God's constancy.

Kathleen Sharps (Cheshire, England)

Daily Bread

Read Matthew 14:13–21
Give me only my daily bread.
Proverbs 30:8 (NIV)

One day as a friend and I were leaving work, he commented, 'I really got my daily bread today.' He explained that he had arrived at work feeling worried and insecure about personal issues. He had prayed for something to happen to help him just get through the day. During the morning, three different people told him what good work he was doing and how pleased they were to have him on their team. These affirmations lifted his spirits and gave him the strength to face his problems outside work too. His final comment was, 'Those three people may not realise it, but they reminded me that God loves me and is guiding me through my troubles.'

The miracle in today's reading appears in all four Gospels and is usually called the feeding of the 5000. But the miracle is even greater than that. Before Jesus fed the crowds physically, he nourished them in other ways. He taught them, encouraged them and healed them. Jesus cared for their complete well-being. When we pray to receive our daily bread, we are asking for more than just physical nourishment. Daily bread also means spiritual, mental and emotional strengthening. God cares about our total well-being and will nourish us daily in many ways.

Prayer: *Dear God, thank you for satisfying all our hungers as we pray, 'Father, hallowed be your name, your kingdom come. Give us each day our daily bread. Forgive us our sins, for we also forgive everyone who sins against us. And lead us not into temptation. Amen.'*

Thought for the day: God is the source of the things that nourish me today.

Gale A. Richards (Iowa, US)

PRAYER FOCUS: THOSE WHOSE BASIC HUMAN NEEDS ARE UNFULFILLED 127
* Luke 11:2–4 (NIV)

Blackberry Pie

Read Luke 6:17–23

I will make them and the region around my hill a blessing; and I will send down the showers in their season; they shall be showers of blessing.
Ezekiel 34:26 (NRSV)

Blackberry bushes grow in our garden like towering green monsters; left unchecked they would engulf it. My husband and I battle them constantly. We cut them back regularly and try to dig out their roots. Yet they grow back, stronger than ever. Every summer we call a truce, as snow-white blossoms give way to plump, juicy blackberries. I pluck them from between the thorns, usually gaining a scratch or two. A few hours later, they have been transformed into blackberry pie. How amazing that something so aggravating can produce such a delicious treat!

I thought about the blackberry bushes as they related to today's reading, in which Jesus talks about truths that seem impossible and contradictory. And Romans 8:28 indicates that bad circumstances can result in a greater good, not only in heaven, but also here on earth. Could that noisy neighbour teach me to be more understanding? Perhaps a frustrating job situation can provide an opportunity to gain new skills. The illness that lays me low could grant me time to rest, read the Bible and pray more deeply. If we look, we can find blessings all around us.

Prayer: *Dear God, help us to see how difficult situations can teach us and draw us closer to you. In Jesus' name, we pray. Amen*

Thought for the day: With God's help, I can look for good in every difficult situation.

Susan Thogerson Maas (Oregon, US)

Saying Yes to God

Read Ephesians 1:3–10

I pray that the eyes of your heart will have enough light to see what is the hope of God's call, what is the richness of God's glorious inheritance.
Ephesians 1:18 (CEB)

After our wedding, my wife and I moved to a new country. During our first church service there, I found an announcement asking for articles for the church magazine. The thought of writing something lingered with me for a few minutes, but then I forgot about it.

The next week when we went to church, the same announcement appeared in the notices. Then the pastor announced that if the Holy Spirit led anyone to write, their contribution would be welcomed. I had never written about the gospel before; I didn't know if I could offer any wisdom to spread God's word. But I listened to the Holy Spirit's call and wrote for the magazine. My articles received praise from the pastor and other members of the congregation. God has beautiful ways of working in our lives and of drawing us closer. He created every life on earth to fulfil a divine purpose. We do not know our full potential, but our Creator does. God waits patiently for us to discover and say yes to that purpose.

Prayer: *Dear Lord, give us hearts willing to follow whenever we hear your call. Amen*

Thought for the day: I can participate in God's creativity.

Deepika Sagar (Rajasthan, India)

The Waitress

Read Romans 12:9–14

Be ye… merciful, as your Father also is merciful.
Luke 6:36 (KJV)

After a long day of driving through the desert, my husband and I spied a little cafe and were anxious to eat and get back on the road. Our young waitress was quite frazzled and distracted. We were disappointed when she brought our dinner, as it was different from what we had ordered. I was still complaining to my husband when she brought our bill. With a quiet sigh, she said, 'I'm sorry for the mix up. I'm just not in the swing of things yet. This is my first day back from maternity leave.' Instantly, my attitude changed. This new mother had left her baby with someone else so she could wait on us—customers with bad attitudes. Instead of complaining to her boss as I had planned, I asked about her baby and gave her a hug. We left a large tip, and I prayed for her as I walked back to the car.

Today's verse says, 'Be merciful.' It does not say to be merciful only if you know the story or if the person 'deserves' it. I certainly learned a lesson from my experience in the cafe in treating people the way Christ would and putting others' needs before my own. The next time I am having difficulty with someone, I am going to stop, take a long look at the situation and ask myself, 'What does this person need?' It may be as simple as a word of encouragement or a prayer.

Prayer: *Dearest Father, help us to be kind to everyone we meet and to show mercy to those we find difficult. In Jesus' name we pray. Amen*

Thought for the day: How can I show Christlike mercy today?

Myla Rae Brueske (Arizona, US)

Small Group Questions

Wednesday 6 January

1. When have you felt as if your life lacked purpose? Describe your situation. What made you feel this way?

2. When you feel lost or purposeless, what do you do? What do you pray? Whom do you turn to for help and advice?

3. Connie writes about the ways her great-nephew helped her to see the beauty and hope in the world around her. Who or what helps you to remain hopeful? What do you see in the world around you that gives you hope for the future?

4. How has your faith in Christ given you a new perspective? What spiritual practices, worship experiences or group studies have helped you to grow in your faith or shift your perspective on an issue?

5. Where have you seen evidence of Christ's presence in your life lately? What helps you to remember to look for him?

Wednesday 13 January

1. How do you think the disciples felt when they were waiting for the Holy Spirit? Do you think they remembered Jesus' promise to them that he would not leave them as orphans?

2. What do Jesus' words mean to you? Do they reassure you and strengthen you? Why or why not?

3. On the day of Pentecost, how were the disciples changed by the coming of the Holy Spirit?

4. Are you aware of the Holy Spirit in your own life? How do you recognise that the Spirit is with you?

5. Has the Holy Spirit changed you in the same way as the disciples were changed? Why? In what ways have you changed?

Wednesday 20 January

1. What do you think of Lin's experience in today's meditation? What was your initial reaction? How can you relate to this story?

2. Recall a time when you felt compassion for someone but were unsure how to respond. What kept you from acting on your feelings of compassion? What finally helped you to act?

3. Who has been a model of compassionate living for you? How does this person show compassion for others? What can you learn from this person's actions?

4. In what ways does your church or community encourage acts of compassion? What kinds of practices help others to show and receive compassion in your community?

5. Who has shown you compassion recently? How did it feel to be the recipient of compassion? To whom do you need to show compassion this week? How will you do this?

Wednesday 27 January

1. Do you struggle with anxiety or worry? Is Romans 8:38–39 a comforting verse for you when you are anxious? What other verses bring you comfort when you are worried?

2. Kelly writes about being anxious when praying aloud. Is praying aloud something that comes easily to you? If praying aloud is difficult for you, why do you think that is? How do you deal with your anxiety?

3. Recall a time when you gave in to your fears. Describe the situation and what made you fearful. How did you feel when you gave in to your fear? Have you faced a similar situation since that experience? How did you respond the second time?

4. In Romans 8:39 Paul assures us that we will never be separated from God's love. Who or what helps you to remember and feel God's love in your daily life? How do you share God's love with others when they are feeling anxious or fearful?

5. When current events or situations in your community create fear and anxiety, how do your church and your church leaders respond? How do they remind you that God is present and always offering love in times of fear?

Wednesday 3 February

1. Have you or a loved one ever experienced a prolonged or debilitating illness? What was that experience like? Whom do you know who is struggling with such an illness at this time?

2. Have you ever prayed with someone from a different denomination or faith tradition? Describe that experience. What surprised you? What was challenging?

3. Recall a time when someone offered a prayer that was particularly powerful or changed the way you think about prayer. What was different about this prayer? What made it powerful? How did that prayer affect your own prayer practice?

4. Arnoldo describes prayer as 'talking with a good friend'. Is this how you experience prayer? If not, describe how prayer feels to you. How are you most comfortable praying?

5. What is the most common way of praying in your church's services? What do you like about this form of prayer? What other ways of praying would you like to try?

Wednesday 10 February

1. Does your church observe Ash Wednesday or are you, like Galina, unfamiliar with this tradition? What do you like about this practice? What more would you like to learn about Ash Wednesday?

2. What practices help to remind you of your need for God? How do these reminders shape the way you interact with others? With God?

3. During Lent, do you usually give up something as a practice of self-denial? Or do you add a practice or discipline to your daily life? How does your practice help you to prepare for Easter or to deepen your faith?

4. How does your church observe Lent or prepare for Easter? Is this an important time for you and your community? Why or why not?

5. Read Isaiah 58:6–7 again. What is your reaction to these verses? Name some of the ways you and your church are living out the 'fast' described here. What other ways can you imagine serving God?

Wednesday 17 February

1. How does Lisa's experience in the prayer meeting resonate with you? Do you recognise yourself in the person who named the request or in the person who thought it was impossible? Why?

2. When you pray, are you more likely to pray for things you feel are 'possible' or things you think are 'impossible'? Give some examples. How does Lisa's story encourage you to think differently about the way you pray?

3. Paul's story is a dramatic example of the way God can change a person's heart. Have you ever experienced a dramatic change of heart? What was the issue? How did God help you to see things differently?

4. What seemingly impossible thing do you want to pray for today? Why does this seem impossible to you?

5. How does your church share prayer requests? How are these requests prayed for? By a prayer group? By individuals? In worship? Do you regularly pray for people in your church? What would help you to be more intentional about praying for others?

Wednesday 24 February

1. When have you been in a relationship where you simply delighted in the presence of the other person? Who was that person? Share some memories of that relationship.

2. Describe your relationship with the parent you are/were closest to. How did this relationship encourage you and shape you?

3. When you pray, how do you address God? Is it helpful for you to think of God as 'father'? Why or why not? What other names for God do you use or find helpful?

4. Jane writes that her son's relationship to his daughter shows her a 'picture of our heavenly Father'. What relationships or experiences in your life have helped you to understand God more fully? How did they reflect God to you?

5. Have you ever felt that you needed to work to please God or earn his love? Why do you think you felt that way? How has your perspective changed, and what helped you to accept God's love and grace?

Wednesday 2 March

1. Scott makes a distinction between attraction and promotion in Jesus' ministry. What do you think he means? Discuss this distinction in more detail and think about other distinctions between Jesus' approach and your own.

2. Think about a time in your life when you approached a situation differently from the way Jesus might have approached it. What was the outcome? How might the outcome have looked different by taking a Christ-centred approach?

3. What does 'do justice… love kindness and… walk humbly before your God' (Micah 6:8) mean? In what practical ways might you live this scripture out?

4. Is sharing Jesus' love with all people an easy task or a hard one? What does making Christian disciples by sharing the love of Jesus with all people look like to you?

5. How does your church encourage you to share the love of Christ? What ministries at your church help others know about God's love?

Wednesday 9 March

1. Recall a time when you had to cope with the illness and/or death of a loved one. What was that experience like for you? From whom did you receive support?

2. When have the prayers of others given you strength to carry a heavy burden? What was it like to know that others were praying for you?

3. In what ways could you support someone who is experiencing circumstances that are similarly difficult to those of Howard?

4. How does it help you to know that even someone like the apostle Paul experienced significant hardships during his life? What other characters in the Bible underwent difficult circumstances? How do these stories encourage you in difficult times?

5. Has there ever been a time in your life when you thought about giving up? Who or what helped you to keep going?

Wednesday 16 March

1. Describe your daily devotional time. Who is present? Where do you sit? What do you do during this time?

2. How important is reading scripture daily to the Christian life? Do you try to read scripture each day? If not, what keeps you from trying? How might including scripture as part of your devotional time shape your entire day?

3. Carla says that each day she prays for some person or part of her life that especially needs God's power. Who in your life needs a prayer for God's power today?

4. How do the stories shared in *The Upper Room* contribute to your devotional time? Name some of the ways you have heard about the magazine being used by individuals, by your community, or by readers around the world.

5. Carla has added her own 'twist' to her devotional time. Do you have any 'twists' of your own?

Wednesday 23 March

1. What images does the word 'light' bring to mind for you? What do you think about the connection Everard makes between light and spiritual renewal? Are there other images that come to mind when thinking about spiritual renewal?

2. How is Holy Communion observed in your faith community? What parts of this practice are particularly meaningful for you?

3. Think about a time when your spiritual life needed renewing. What sources did you draw on for renewal? In what ways could you help others who are also in need of renewal?

4. What do Jesus' words 'I am the light of the world. Whoever follows me will never walk in darkness, but will have the light of life' mean to you?

5. Everard writes, 'Spiritual renewal comes through… acts of love and service.' How does your church encourage you to engage in acts of love and service? Where have you taken part in such acts recently?

Wednesday 30 March

1. Have you ever had an experience similar to John's? What challenges does a situation such as this present? How did you feel after the experience?

2. What does it mean to you to 'love your neighbour as yourself'? In what ways might this be difficult?

3. How do you respond to John's statement, 'Jesus lived a life of sacrifice and compassion, and he calls us to do the same'? What does living a life of sacrifice and compassion mean to you? Who in your life has shown you how to live a life?

4. Think of the neighbour who is the hardest for you to love. In what ways could you make a sacrifice for or extend compassion to this person?

5. Identify some neighbours who are in need in your community. How can you reach out and help them meet some of their needs?

Wednesday 6 April

1. Have you experienced a devastating loss in your life? If so, describe what that was like. How did you cope with the experience?

2. How does your community support people in times of despair, doubt, sorrow and anger? Do you see other ways you or your community could help?

3. What does 2 Corinthians 12:9 mean to you? What do you think Paul is saying when he writes, 'I will boast all the more gladly of my weaknesses, so that the power of Christ may dwell in me'?

4. Can you recall a time when your faith has been tested? What was it that tested your faith? What was this like for you?

5. Is your faith today as strong as you would like it to be? If so, what sustains your faith? If not, what would help you strengthen your faith? Name some specific acts of love and service that can lead to spiritual renewal.

Wednesday 13 April

1. In what circumstances are you most likely to lose your perspective? What helps you keep your perspective?

2. How does being aware of God's presence shape your daily life? In what parts of your daily life can you work to become more aware of his presence?

3. Think of a time when you were so busy that you failed to notice how God was at work in a situation. Who or what helped you to recognise God's presence in that situation?

4. When has someone pointed something out to you that you would not have seen without his or her help? In addition to Mark 4:11–12, are there other scripture passages that come to mind when you think back on this experience?

5. Think about a time when you gained an insight or new perspective on something and had to tell others about it because it was too good to keep to yourself. Do you feel this way about sharing the good news?

Wednesday 20 April

1. Do you have a family memento that is meaningful to you in the same way the cane is to Debra? What stories are associated with it?

2. If you were to write a meditation on an object that brings you comfort, what would it be and what would you say about it?

3. What passages of scripture bring you comfort in times of grief, doubt and fear? Are there one or two passages in particular that you lean on most often?

4. Can you think of a time when you were in a 'dark valley' but a friend, companion or colleague walked through it with you? How would the experience have been different if you had had to go through it alone?

5. Who needs your prayers of hope and healing today? What are you currently dealing with for which you would ask the prayers of others?

Wednesday 27 April

1. How often do you thank God for your daily blessings? What blessings can you thank him for today?

2. When was the last time someone reminded you of God's love? Who in your community can you remind of his love today?

3. What nourishes your spiritual life? Does your spiritual nourishment come from reading scripture, prayer, keeping a journal, a walk in the countryside or some combination of these? Are there other practices that give you nourishment?

4. Name some of the ways Jesus cares for us each day. What other connections do you see between Jesus' feeding the 5000 and his care for us?

5. What does the writer of Proverbs mean when he says, 'Give me only my daily bread'?

Dust and Glory

Daily Bible readings from Ash Wednesday to Easter Day

David Runcorn

Lent is one of the three 40-day 'seasons' in the church's year, besides Advent and the period from Easter to Pentecost. The name itself, Lent, derives from an ancient word meaning 'spring' or 'long', referring to the time of year when days are beginning to lengthen and the world is turning from winter cold and dark to the warmth and promise of spring. During this time, the church calls us to a special period of prayer, self-examination and teaching—and this book has been written to accompany you through that period, a time of turning from winter to spring, from death to life.

Dust and Glory ranges across the whole business of living and believing, where the questions are as important as the answers and may call us to deep heart-searching. The goal is always to draw us to authentic faith—a way of living and believing that is real and vulnerable, strong in knowing its limits, rooted in joy and wonder, blessed with the healing and merciful presence of God. Such faith acknowledges both the dust of our mortality and the glory that keeps breaking in with unexpected life, hope and new beginnings.

ISBN 978 0 85746 357 9   £7.99
To order a copy of this book, please turn to the order form on page 159.

Postcards from Heaven

Words and pictures to help you hear from God

Ellie Hart

'My heart's desire is that this book could become a place where you can encounter our wonderful, beautiful, untameable, passionate, loving God and hear him speak directly to you, whatever your circumstances.'

Writer and artist Ellie Hart has created a series of 'postcards from heaven'—her own paintings linked to short, thought-provoking reflections, to help all who long to hear more clearly from God, especially when going through seasons of change and uncertainty.

ISBN 978 0 85746 427 9   £7.99

To order a copy of this book, please turn to the order form on page 159.

Resourcing Rural Ministry

Practical insights for mission

Jill Hopkinson (ed.)

Resourcing Rural Ministry offers an in-depth exploration of the key aspects, challenges and opportunities of mission in a rural church. Relevant for ordained and lay leaders alike, the book covers subjects ranging from encouraging evangelism in a multi-church group to making best use of church buildings. Containing a wealth of real-life case studies and suggestions for follow-up, this ecumenical publication draws on the expertise and resources of the Arthur Rank Centre (ARC), which has served the spiritual and practical needs of the rural Christian community for over 40 years.

This book contributes to ARC's Germinate programme of training, development and support for rural multi-church groups of all denominations.

ISBN 978 0 85746 262 6   £8.99
To order a copy of this book, please turn to the order form on page 159.

Believe in Miracles

A spiritual journey of positive change

Carmel Thomason

Believe in Miracles is a 40-day journey into a world of possibility. Focusing on small practical steps, you are invited to follow a series of short exercises that will help bring about lasting changes in your life, leading to a more prayerful, contented and connected state of being. By looking for the good and focusing on actions to take now, you will learn to view differently your daily circumstances, your relationship with God, and your relationships with others, bringing something of the ways of heaven to earth.

ISBN 978 0 85746 420 0   £7.99
To order a copy of this book, please turn to the order form on page 159.

How to encourage Bible reading in your church

BRF has been helping individuals connect with the Bible for over 90 years. We want to support churches as they seek to encourage church members into regular Bible reading.

Order a Bible reading resources pack

This pack is designed to give your church the tools to publicise our Bible reading notes. It includes:

- Sample Bible reading notes for your congregation to try.
- Publicity resources, including a poster.
- A church magazine feature about Bible reading notes.

The pack is free, but we welcome a £5 donation to cover the cost of postage. If you require a pack to be sent outside the UK or require a specific number of sample Bible reading notes, please contact us for postage costs. More information about what the current pack contains is available on our website.

How to order and find out more

- Visit **www.biblereadingnotes.org.uk/for-churches/**
- Telephone BRF on 01865 319700 between 9.15 am and 5.30 pm.
- Write to us at BRF, 15 The Chambers, Vineyard, Abingdon, OX14 3FE.

Keep informed about our latest initiatives

We are continuing to develop resources to help churches encourage people into regular Bible reading, wherever they are on their journey. Join our email list at **www.biblereadingnotes.org.uk/helpingchurches/** to stay informed about the latest initiatives that your church could benefit from.

Introduce a friend to our notes

We can send information about our notes and current prices for you to pass on. Please contact us.

Subscriptions

The Upper Room is published in January, May and September.

Individual subscriptions

The subscription rate for orders for 4 or fewer copies includes postage and packing: THE UPPER ROOM annual individual subscription   £16.20

Church subscriptions

Orders for 5 copies or more, sent to ONE address, are post free:
THE UPPER ROOM annual church subscription   £13.05

Please do not send payment with order for a church subscription. We will send an invoice with your first order.

Please note that the annual billing period for church subscriptions runs from 1 May to 30 April.

Copies of the notes may also be obtained from Christian bookshops.

Single copies of *The Upper Room* will cost £4.35. Prices valid until 30 April 2017.

Giant print version

The Upper Room is available in giant print for the visually impaired, from:

Torch Trust for the Blind
Torch House
Torch Way,
Northampton Road
Market Harborough
LE16 9HL

Tel: 01858 438260
www.torchtrust.org

Individual Subscriptions

☐ I would like to take out a subscription myself (complete your name and address details only once)

☐ I would like to give a gift subscription (please complete both name and address sections below)

Your name...

Your address...

....Postcode...

Your telephone number..

Gift subscription name...

Gift subscription address...

....Postcode...

Gift message (20 words max)..

....

Please send *The Upper Room* beginning with the May 2016 / September 2016 / January 2017 issue: (delete as applicable)

THE UPPER ROOM ☐ £16.20

Please complete the payment details below and send, with appropriate payment, to: BRF, 15 The Chambers, Vineyard, Abingdon OX14 3FE

Total enclosed £ .... (cheques should be made payable to 'BRF')

Payment by ☐ cheque ☐ postal order ☐ Visa ☐ Mastercard ☐ Switch

Card no: | | | | | | | | | | | | | | | | | | | |

Expires: | | | | Security code: | | | |

Issue no (Switch): | | | |

Signature (essential if paying by credit/Switch card) ....

☐ Please do not send me further information about BRF publications

☐ Please send me a Bible reading resources pack to encourage Bible reading in my church

BRF is a Registered Charity

Church Subscriptions

☐ Please send me ... copies of *The Upper Room* May 2016 / September 2016 / January 2017 issue (delete as applicable)

Name...

Address ....

....Postcode...

Telephone ....

Email..

Please send this completed form to:
BRF, 15 The Chambers, Vineyard, Abingdon OX14 3FE

Please do not send payment with this order. We will send an invoice with your first order.

Christian bookshops: All good Christian bookshops stock BRF publications. For your nearest stockist, please contact BRF.

Telephone: The BRF office is open between 09.15 and 17.30. To place your order, telephone 01865 319700; fax 01865 319701.

Web: Visit www.brf.org.uk

☐ Please send me a Bible reading resources pack to encourage Bible reading in my church

BRF is a Registered Charity

ORDER FORM

REF	TITLE	PRICE	QTY	TOTAL
357 9	Dust and Glory	£7.99		
427 9	Postcards from Heaven	£7.99		
262 6	Resourcing Rural Ministry	£8.99		
420 0	Believe in Miracles	£7.99		
		Postage and packing		
		Donation		
		TOTAL		

POSTAGE AND PACKING CHARGES				
Order value	UK	Europe	Economy (Surface)	Standard (Air)
Under £7.00	£1.25	£3.00	£3.50	£5.50
£7.00–£29.99	£2.25	£5.50	£6.50	£10.00
£30.00 and over	FREE	prices on request		

Name _____ Account Number _____

Address _____

_____ Postcode _____

Telephone Number_____

Email _____

Payment by: ❑ Cheque ❑ Mastercard ❑ Visa ❑ Postal Order ❑ Maestro

Card no ❑❑❑❑ ❑❑❑❑ ❑❑❑❑ ❑❑❑❑ ❑❑❑

Valid from ❑❑❑❑ Expires ❑❑❑❑ Issue no. ❑❑❑

Security code* ❑❑❑ *Last 3 digits on the reverse of the card. Shaded boxes for
ESSENTIAL IN ORDER TO PROCESS YOUR ORDER   Maestro use only

Signature _____ Date _____

All orders must be accompanied by the appropriate payment.

Please send your completed order form to:
BRF, 15 The Chambers, Vineyard, Abingdon OX14 3FE
Tel. 01865 319700 / Fax. 01865 319701 Email: enquiries@brf.org.uk

❑ Please send me further information about BRF publications.

Available from your local Christian bookshop.   BRF is a Registered Charity

About

brf:

BRF is a registered charity and also a limited company, and has been in existence since 1922. Through all that we do—producing resources, providing training, working face-to-face with adults and children, and via the web— we work to resource individuals and church communities in their Christian discipleship through the Bible, prayer and worship.

Our Barnabas children's team works with primary schools and churches to help children under 11, and the adults who work with them, to explore Christianity creatively and to bring the Bible alive.

To find out more about BRF and its core activities and ministries, visit:

www.brf.org.uk
www.brfonline.org.uk
www.biblereadingnotes.org.uk
www.barnabasinschools.org.uk
www.barnabasinchurches.org.uk
www.faithinhomes.org.uk
www.messychurch.org.uk

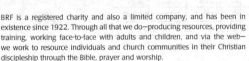

If you have any questions about BRF and our work, please email us at

enquiries@brf.org.uk